Cannabis Use

ISSUES

Volume 186

Series Editor

Lisa Firth

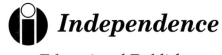

Independence

Educational Publishers
Cambridge

First published by Independence
The Studio, High Green
Great Shelford
Cambridge CB22 5EG
England

© Independence 2010

British Library Cataloguing in Publication Data
Cannabis use – (Issues ; v.186)
1. Cannabis 2. Marijuana 3. Marijuana abuse
4. Marijuana – Law and legislation
I. Series II. Firth, Lisa
362.2'95-dc22

ISBN-13: 978 1 86168 527 8

Printed in Great Britain
MWL Print Group Ltd

Cover
The illustration on the front cover is by
Angelo Madrid.

CONTENTS

Chapter One: The Effects of Cannabis

Chapter Two: Cannabis and the Law

Useful information for readers

Dear Reader,

Issues: Cannabis Use

Cannabis is the most widely-used illegal substance in Britain. Users say it helps them to relax: however, there are worries that smoking the drug can trigger mental health problems, with highly potent 'skunk' strains causing particular concern. This book looks at the cannabis debate, including issues such as reclassification, cannabis use for medical reasons and cannabis-related health problems.

The purpose of *Issues*

Cannabis Use is the one hundred and eighty-sixth volume in the **Issues** series. The aim of this series is to offer up-to-date information about important issues in our world. Whether you are a regular reader or new to the series, we do hope you find this book a useful overview of the many and complex issues involved in the topic. This title replaces an older volume in the **Issues** series, Volume 128: **The Cannabis Issue,** which is now out of print.

Titles in the **Issues** series are resource books designed to be of especial use to those undertaking project work or requiring an overview of facts, opinions and information on a particular subject, particularly as a prelude to undertaking their own research.

The information in this book is not from a single author, publication or organisation; the value of this unique series lies in the fact that it presents information from a wide variety of sources, including:

⇨ Government reports and statistics
⇨ Newspaper articles and features
⇨ Information from think-tanks and policy institutes
⇨ Magazine features and surveys
⇨ Website material
⇨ Literature from lobby groups and charitable organisations.*

Critical evaluation

Because the information reprinted here is from a number of different sources, readers should bear in mind the origin of the text and whether the source is likely to have a particular bias or agenda when presenting information (just as they would if undertaking their own research). It is hoped that, as you read about the many aspects of the issues explored in this book, you will critically evaluate the information presented. It is important that you decide whether you are being presented with facts or opinions. Does the writer give a biased or an unbiased report? If an opinion is being expressed, do you agree with the writer?

Cannabis Use offers a useful starting point for those who need convenient access to information about the many issues involved. However, it is only a starting point. Following each article is a URL to the relevant organisation's website, which you may wish to visit for further information.

Kind regards,

Lisa Firth
Editor, **Issues** series

** Please note that Independence Publishers has no political affiliations or opinions on the topics covered in the **Issues** series, and any views quoted in this book are not necessarily those of the publisher or its staff.*

ISSUES TODAY
A RESOURCE FOR KEY STAGE 3

Younger readers can also benefit from the thorough editorial process which characterises the **Issues** series with our resource books for 11- to 14-year-old students, **Issues Today**. In addition to containing information from a wide range of sources, rewritten with this age group in mind, **Issues Today** titles also feature comprehensive glossaries, an accessible and attractive layout and handy tasks and assignments which can be used in class, for homework or as a revision aid. In addition, these titles are fully photocopiable. For more information, please visit our website (www.independence. co.uk).

Cannabis

Information from FRANK

Cannabis is the most widely used illegal drug in Britain. Made from parts of the cannabis plant, it's a naturally occurring drug. It is a mild sedative (often causing a chilled-out feeling or actual sleepiness) and it's also a mild hallucinogen (meaning you may experience a state where you see objects and reality in a distorted way and may even hallucinate). The main active compound in cannabis is tetrahydrocannabinol (THC).

Cannabis is illegal; it's a class B drug

Slang

Street names for drugs can vary around the country and with different forms: Bhang, black, blast, blow, blunts, Bob Hope, bush, dope, draw, ganja, grass, hash, hashish, hemp, herb, marijuana, pot, puff, Northern Lights, resin, sensi, sinsemilla, shit, skunk, smoke, soap, spliff, wacky backy, weed, zero. Some names are based on where it comes from... Afghan, homegrown, Moroccan, etc.

The effects
⇨ Some people may feel chilled out, relaxed and happy,' while others have one puff and feel sick.
⇨ Others get the giggles and may become talkative.
⇨ Hunger pangs are common and are known as 'getting the munchies'.
⇨ Users may become more aware of their senses or get a feeling of slowing of time, which are due to its hallucinogenic effects.

Stronger 'joints' (e.g. typically when skunk or sinsemilla is used) may have more powerful effects. Some users may moderate this effect by actually inhaling and using less

strong cannabis; but others may find it becomes tempting to 'binge smoke' them.

The regular use of cannabis is known to be associated with an increase in the risk of later developing psychotic illnesses including schizophrenia. If the recent increase in availability of stronger forms of cannabis does lead to an increase in total use by some people, this might also lead to an increase in their future risk of developing mental health problems. Nobody knows the answer to this question yet...

Chances of getting hooked
As with other drugs, dependence on cannabis is influenced by a number of factors, including how long you've been using it, how much you use and whether you are just more prone to become dependent. You may find you have difficulty stopping regular use

and you may experience psychological and physical withdrawals when you do stop. The withdrawals can include cravings for cannabis, irritability, mood changes, appetite disturbance, weight loss, difficulty sleeping and even sweating, shaking and diarrhoea in some people.

If you've only been using for a short while there should be no problem stopping but with continued regular use of cannabis, this can become more difficult. You're also at risk of getting addicted to nicotine if you roll your spliffs with tobacco.

The law
⇨ Cannabis is illegal; it's a class B drug.
⇨ If you're caught with cannabis the police will always take action.
Possession:
⇨ If you're caught with even a small amount of cannabis the police will confiscate the drug and you can be arrested. What the police will do depends on the circumstances and how old you are.
⇨ Usually, you'll get a cannabis

warning if you're 18 and over. If you're under 18, you'll get a reprimand and your parent or guardian will also be contacted. The police are more likely to arrest you if you are blatantly smoking in public and/or have been caught with cannabis before.

⇨ If you're under 18, the second time you get caught you're likely to get a final warning and be referred to a Youth Offending Team. If you're 18 and over, the second time you get caught you're likely to get a Penalty Notice of Disorder, which is an on-the-spot fine of £80. This gets logged on the Police National Computer.

⇨ Regardless of how old you are, if you're caught with cannabis for a third time it's likely you will be arrested.

Even hardcore smokers can become anxious, panicky, suspicious or paranoid

⇨ If you continue to break the law, you can end up with a criminal record which could affect your chances of getting a job. It could also affect whether you can go on holiday to some countries.

⇨ The maximum penalty for possession is five years in prison plus an unlimited fine.

Supply:

⇨ Dealing is a very serious offence.

⇨ In the eyes of the law, this includes giving drugs to friends.

⇨ People who grow cannabis in their homes or carry large amounts on them also risk being charged with intent to supply.

⇨ The maximum penalty for supply is 14 years in prison plus an unlimited fine.

Did you know?

⇨ Drug driving is as illegal as drink driving. You could go to prison, get a heavy fine or be disqualified.

⇨ Allowing people to take cannabis in your house or any other premises is illegal. If the police catch someone smoking cannabis

in a club they can prosecute the landlord, club owner or person holding the party.

⇨ Using cannabis to relieve pain is also an offence. Possession is illegal whatever you're using it for.

Appearance and use

Cannabis comes in different forms.

Hash is a black or brown lump made from the resin of the plant. It's quite often squidgy. In the past, this was the commonest form of cannabis in the UK, but this is no longer the case.

Much less common is cannabis oil, made by separating the resin from the cannabis plant using various solvents. It is a sticky, dark honey-coloured oil.

Herbal cannabis (grass or weed) is made from the dried leaves and flowering parts of the female plant and looks like tightly packed dried herbs.

Recently, there has been an increased availability of strong herbal cannabis, containing on average two to three times the amount of the active compound, tetrahydrocannabinol or THC, as compared to the traditional imported 'weed'. This strong cannabis includes: 'sinsemilla' (a bud grown in the absence of male plants and which has no seeds); 'homegrown'; 'skunk', which has a characteristic strong smell; and imported 'netherweed'. Strong cannabis is grown through processes that can include selective breeding, use of hydroponics and special heating and lighting techniques.

Most people mix cannabis with tobacco and smoke it as a spliff or a joint. Some people put it in a bong or a type of pipe. And others make tea with it or stick it in food like cakes or 'cannabis cookies'.

Cost

Prices can vary from region to region. The prices given here are an average of street prices reported from 20 different parts of Britain. Grass is usually more expensive: currently between £90 to £130, with resin (hash) at around £50 per ounce.

Purity

When thinking about the purity of cannabis, we can consider two

separate areas: first, the 'strength' of the unadulterated product (i.e. how much THC it contains), and second how much it is 'cut' or contaminated.

As a cannabis user, it may not be possible to tell whether a particular sample of 'skunk' or 'homegrown' or 'sinsemilla' will have a higher potency than an equal amount of traditional herbal cannabis – because the actual potencies of different products overlap substantially. From a health perspective, it is important to understand that the long-term impact of smoking these higher potency forms is not yet clear, but might include an increase in the risk of later developing psychotic illnesses including schizophrenia or possibly an increased risk of developing dependence. Nobody yet knows the answer on these points.

The potency of herbal cannabis decreases over time in storage and is affected by what parts of the plant have been included in the product. Hence, a user has little guarantee about the 'intensity of the high'. The intensity of the smell of skunk or its appearance may not act as reliable guide to the actual strength either.

In recent years, herbal cannabis with a gritty texture was found from suppliers who had sprayed glass on the product, possibly to alter its look and weight.

Cannabis resin sold as hash, especially the 'Soap Bar' variety, is usually cut with other substances to increase the bulk and thus to increase the supplier's profit. The contaminants may include a variety of substances,

with reports of henna, turpentine, boot polish, animal poo, and even tranquillisers. These impurities are then smoked and inhaled along with the cannabis resin.

The risks

⇨ Even hardcore smokers can become anxious, panicky, suspicious or paranoid.

⇨ Cannabis affects your coordination, which is one of the reasons why drug driving is just as illegal as drink driving.

⇨ Some people think cannabis is harmless just because it's a plant – but it isn't harmless. Cannabis, like tobacco, has lots of chemical 'nasties', which can cause lung disease and possibly cancer with long-term or heavy use, especially as it is often mixed with tobacco and smoked without a filter. It can also make asthma worse, and cause wheezing in non-asthma sufferers.

⇨ Cannabis itself can affect many different systems in the body, including the heart: it increases the heart rate and can affect blood pressure.

⇨ If you've a history of mental health problems, then taking cannabis is not a good idea: it can cause paranoia in the short term, but in those with a pre-existing psychotic illness, such as schizophrenia, it can contribute to relapse.

⇨ If you use cannabis and have a family background of mental illness, such as schizophrenia, you may be at increased risk of developing a psychotic illness.

⇨ It is reported that frequent use of cannabis can cut a man's sperm count, reduce sperm motility, and can suppress ovulation in women and so may affect fertility.

⇨ If you're pregnant, smoking cannabis frequently may have some association with the risk of the baby being born smaller than expected.

⇨ Regular, heavy use makes it difficult to learn and concentrate. Some people begin to feel tired all the time and can't seem to get motivated.

⇨ Some users may want to buy strong herbal cannabis to get 'a bigger high' but unpleasant reactions can be more powerful when you use strong cannabis, and it is possible that using strong cannabis repeatedly could lead in time to more users experiencing harmful effects such as dependence or being more at risk of developing the mental health effects.

⇨ The above information is reprinted with kind permission from FRANK. Visit www.talktofrank.com for more. You can telephone FRANK on 0800 776600. If you are deaf or hard of hearing you can also textphone FRANK on 0800 9178765, or text a question to them on 82111.

Cannabis controversy

Information from politics.co.uk

What is cannabis?

Cannabis is a durable hemp plant. The cannabis plant can be used to produce a number of products including seeds, pulp and medicine. The pulp is used as fuel and to make paper, the seed is used in foods, and the oil from the seed can be used as a base for paints and varnishes. The blossoms and leaves of the hemp plant produce a sticky resin, which has historically been used for a variety of medicinal purposes, and for just as long for recreational drug use.

The compound that gives cannabis its mind-altering properties is delta-9-tetrahydrocannabinol, known as THC.

Background

Early explorers and botanists placed the origins of the cannabis or hemp plant in central Asia.

The plant was used in the empires of ancient China about 5,000 years ago, and has also been used as part of many religious practices.

In more recent history, cannabis has been used by writers and others artists as a source of inspiration and to aid imagination. For example, the books *Alice in Wonderland* and *Through the Looking Glass* were thought to be written while Lewis Carroll was using cannabis.

In the early 1900s, cannabis was popular both as a recreational and a medicinal compound and it is rumoured to have been given to Queen Victoria by her doctor to relieve period pain. The development of superior alternatives, such as the invention of the syringe for rapid drug inducement and the development of aspirin, led to the reduced use of cannabis in medicine.

Cannabis was first made illegal in the UK in 1928. The 1971 Misuse of Drugs Act was later introduced

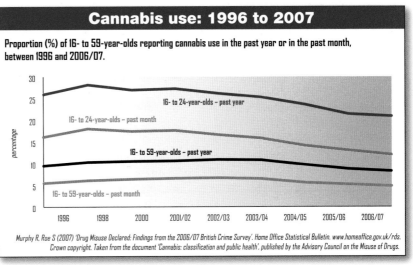

Cannabis use: 1996 to 2007

Proportion (%) of 16- to 59-year-olds reporting cannabis use in the past year or in the past month, between 1996 and 2006/07.

16- to 24-year-olds – past year

16- to 24-year-olds – past month

16- to 59-year-olds – past year

16- to 59-year-olds – past month

Murphy R, Roe S (2007) 'Drug Misuse Declared: Findings from the 2006/07 British Crime Survey'. Home Office Statistical Bulletin. www.homeoffice.gov.uk/rds. Crown copyright. Taken from the document 'Cannabis: classification and public health', published by the Advisory Council on the Misuse of Drugs.

to provide guidance on controlled drugs, and cannabis was classified as a 'class B' drug.

There has subsequently been a change in the Government's stance on cannabis, largely in response to changing public perception towards the drug.

In the early 1900s, cannabis was popular both as a recreational and a medicinal compound and it is rumoured to have been given to Queen Victoria by her doctor to relieve period pain

---

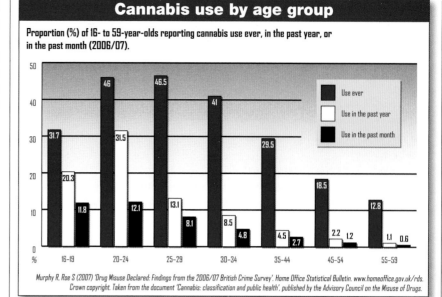

Cannabis use by age group

Proportion (%) of 16- to 59-year-olds reporting cannabis use ever, in the past year, or in the past month (2006/07).

Use ever
Use in the past year
Use in the past month

Murphy R. Roe S (2007) 'Drug Misuse Declared: Findings from the 2006/07 British Crime Survey'. Home Office Statistical Bulletin. www.homeoffice.gov.uk/rds. Crown copyright. Taken from the document 'Cannabis: classification and public health'. published by the Advisory Council on the Misuse of Drugs.

In 2001, the Commons' Home Affairs Select Committee carried out a major study into drugs, titled *The Government's Drugs Policy: Is It Working?*. The report called for a major shake-up of the Government's drugs policy, concentrating on education and harm reduction for users rather than criminal sanctions. The report also recommended the re-classification of cannabis to a class C drug. A report by the House of Lords Science and Technology Committee in 2001 recommended the use of cannabis for medicinal purposes.

In 2002, Home Secretary David Blunkett announced that he might permit the medical use of cannabis if clinical trials of the drug were successful.

In January 2004, cannabis was downgraded to a class C drug across the country.

In March 2005, Home Secretary Charles Clarke asked the advisory council on the misuse of drugs (ACMD) to examine new evidence on the harmfulness of cannabis and consider whether this changed their assessment of cannabis as a class C drug. In a report in January 2006, the council concluded that cannabis should remain a class C drug, and the Home Office accepted this.

However, the Home Secretary said a programme of public education was needed to raise understanding about the implications of cannabis consumption. The campaign was delivered in partnership with the police and also aimed to publicise the penalties for dealing, producing, and using cannabis.

After ten years of liberalising attitudes and policy under the Labour Government, the Prime Minister Gordon Brown signalled in 2007 that he would consider reclassifying cannabis as a class B drug. Ministers appeared sympathetic to evidence that cannabis was getting stronger, due to the greater availability of skunk, and the reported links between cannabis use and mental illness.

The renewed debate sparked a flurry of confessions by senior ministers that they had smoked the drug in their youth. Among them was the woman in charge of the review, the Home Secretary Jacqui Smith.

In May 2008, the Government announced its decision to reclassify cannabis as a class B drug under the Misuse of Drugs Act 1971. Following debates in both Houses of Parliament, reclassification came into effect on 26 January 2009.

Controversies

Whether cannabis should be legalised, decriminalised or reclassified are all controversial issues, as are any Government attempts to reform the law on drug use.

Debates about drugs have often lumped 'soft drugs' such as cannabis together with 'hard drugs' like heroin and cocaine, if not by ascribing the same physiological and social effects to each, then by regarding the soft drugs as a 'gateway' to hard drug use.

Medical opinion remains divided over the effects of cannabis on users' mental and physical health and on its addictive properties.

In 2001, the Government began a major policy shift on cannabis by conducting a trial in Lambeth, South London, for dealing with cannabis possession offences. Officers in the area would no longer arrest individuals for possession but instead issue a verbal warning and confiscate the substance. The rationale was that by relaxing the current procedures police would be freed up to deal with more serious offences.

However, the scheme caused outcry among some religious and community groups who claimed the Government had 'gone soft' on drugs, sending the wrong message out to youngsters and letting dealers 'get away with it'.

But advocates of legalising cannabis say that its widespread use undermines the law and criminalises otherwise law-abiding users. They also call for a change in the law on libertarian grounds and refute the suggestion that cannabis use leads to harder drugs.

Although it is questionable whether cannabis use always leads to hard drug abuse, drug dealers rarely discriminate between the varieties, and many fear that decriminalisation of cannabis will prop up hard drug dealing and associated organised crime.

The Government's decision in 2008 to reclassify cannabis as a class B drug was highly controversial, not least because it rejected the findings of a review by the Advisory Council for the Misuse of Drugs carried out at the request of the Prime Minister.

The ACMD report, *Cannabis: Classification and Public Health*, published in May 2008, concluded that 'after a most careful scrutiny of the totality of the available evidence, the majority of the council's members consider - based on its harmfulness to individuals and society - that cannabis should remain a class C substance.'

Nevertheless, the ACMD emphasised that in their opinion the use of cannabis was 'a significant public health issue' which could 'unquestionably cause harm to individuals and society'. But the council advised that public health strategies developed under the auspices of the UK's chief medical officers, which were designed to minimise cannabis use, would be far more effective than reclassification or criminal justice measures.

The Government accepted 20 of the report's 21 recommendations, rejecting recommendation 3, that 'Cannabis should remain a class C drug'. Reclassification of cannabis to class B was, the Government said, 'a preventative measure' which 'takes account of its known risks to health as well as the potential long-term impacts on health where the evidence is not conclusive'.

It added: 'Reclassifying cannabis to class B will reinforce our national message that cannabis is harmful and illegal, and will help to drive the enforcement priorities to reverse the massive growth in commercial cultivation.'

Disagreements between the Government and the ACMD over drugs classification continued, culminating in the dismissal of the ACMD chair, Professor David Nutt, in November 2009, following his frequent public criticisms of the Government's drugs policy. Two of his colleagues then resigned from the ACMD: Dr Les King, and Marion Walker, the Royal Pharmaceutical Society's representative on the council.

Statistics

As a class B drug, current penalties for cannabis are as follows:

Penalties for supply, dealing, production and trafficking

The maximum penalty is 14 years imprisonment.

Penalties for possession

The maximum penalty increases from two years to five years imprisonment.

Adults in possession of cannabis

If caught in possession of cannabis, as well as considering arrest and confiscating the drug, police are likely to: give a cannabis warning for a first offence of possession; give a Penalty Notice for Disorder - this is an on-the-spot fine of £80 for a second offence; make an arrest if it is the third offence of having been caught with cannabis - this could lead to conviction and a criminal record.

Young people in possession of cannabis

A young person found to be in possession of cannabis will be arrested and taken to a police station where they can receive a reprimand, final warning or charge depending on the seriousness of the offence.

Following one reprimand, any further offence will lead to a final warning or charge. Any further offence following a warning will normally result in criminal charges. After a final warning, the young offender must be referred to a Youth Offending Team to arrange a rehabilitation programme.

This police enforcement is consistent with the structured framework for early juvenile offending established under the Crime and Disorder Act 1998.

Source: Home Office - 2009

Quotes

'Gordon Brown comes into office and soon after that he starts saying absurd things like cannabis is lethal... it has to be a class B drug. He has made his mind up. We went back, we looked at the evidence, we said, "No, no, there is no extra evidence of harm, it's still a class C drug." He said, "Tough, it's going to be class B."

'There's no point in having drug laws that are meaningless and arbitrary just because politicians find it useful and expedient occasionally to come down hard on drugs. That's undermining the whole purpose of the drugs laws.'
Former ACMD chair Professor David Nutt, speaking to the BBC - November 2009

'It was right to reclassify cannabis... It's right also to say that drugs can cause such damage, particularly when dealers are pushing drugs on young people and making them victims of a cruel trade... I think everybody knows lives that have been ruined because of drugs.

'It's very important that we say yes, we take scientific advice seriously and will never ignore it, but yes, also, it is right that the people who make the final decisions and are accountable to Parliament for them are the Home Secretary in this case or in other cases the Health Secretary or myself.'
Prime Minister Gordon Brown, speaking to the London Evening Standard - November 2009

⇨ The above information is reprinted with kind permission from politics.co.uk. Visit www.politics.co.uk for more information.

© Adfero

... LEWIS CARROLL WASN'T USING SKUNK CANNABIS WHEN HE WROTE ALICE IN WONDERLAND ...

OH - YEAH, OTHERWISE THE WHITE RABBIT WOULD HAVE BEEN A SKUNK, HEY!!

Risks of cannabis use

Why should we care about cannabis?

Approximately four per cent of the world's adults – some 162 million people – use cannabis at least once in the course of a year, making it the world's most widely used illicit drug. In some countries, more than half of all young people have tried it. In spite of this high rate of usage, many basic facts about cannabis remain obscure. Of particular concern are the recent growth in the drug's potency, and mounting questions about the role of cannabis in mental illnesses.

In recent years, research has demonstrated that cannabis is becoming more potent. Studies done in key markets such as the Netherlands, the US and Canada, for example, have shown that the potency of sinsemilla cannabis, made from the unfertilised buds of the female plant, has doubled. The market for this high-potency, indoor-produced variety appears to be growing in many key consumption countries. As the drug grows stronger, users consequently experience more powerful – and dangerous – psychological effects. Emerging research indicates that cannabis consumption may have greater mental health implications than previously believed.

Although it is often seen as a less harmful drug, cannabis use poses several health risks. Even when used only once, cannabis may lead to panic attacks, paranoia, psychotic symptoms and other acute negative effects. The drug may also precipitate psychosis in vulnerable individuals and intensify symptoms in diagnosed schizophrenics. As it is mostly smoked and contains high levels of tar, cannabis additionally puts users at an increased risk of lung cancer and other respiratory diseases.

The risk of becoming dependent on cannabis is also higher than most casual users suspect. Regular users risk developing psychological dependence to the point where they cannot quit even when the drug use starts to negatively impact other areas of their lives, such as work and personal relations. Around nine per cent of those who try cannabis are unable to stop using it, and demand for treatment for cannabis-related problems has increased in recent years in the US and Europe.
25 April 2008

⇨ The above information is reprinted with kind permission from the United Nations Office on Drugs and Crime. Visit www.unodc.org for more information on this and other related topics.
© United Nations Office on Drugs and Crime

Impact of cannabis on bones 'changes with age'

Information from Arthritis Research Campaign

Scientists investigating the effects of cannabis on bone health have found that its impact varies dramatically with age.

The study has found that although cannabis could reduce bone strength in young people, it may protect against osteoporosis, a weakening of the bones, in later life.

The team at the University of Edinburgh has shown that a molecule found naturally in the body, which can be activated by cannabis – called the type 1 cannabinoid receptor (CB1) – is key to the development of osteoporosis.

It is known that when CB1 comes into contact with cannabis it has an impact on bone regeneration, but until now it was not clear whether the drug had a positive or negative effect.

Researchers, funded by the Arthritis Research Campaign, investigated this by studying mice that lacked the CB1 receptor. The scientists then used compounds – similar to those in cannabis – that activated the CB1 receptor. They found that compounds increased the rate at which bone tissue was destroyed in the young.

The study also showed, however, that the same compounds decreased bone loss in older mice and prevented the accumulation of fat in the bones, which is known to occur in humans with osteoporosis. The results are published in *Cell Metabolism*.

Osteoporosis affects up to 30 per cent of women and 12 per cent of men at some point in life.

Stuart Ralston, the Arthritis Research Campaign Professor of Rheumatology at the University of Edinburgh, who led the study, said: 'This is an exciting step forward, but we must recognise that these are early results and more tests are needed on the effects of cannabis in humans to determine how the effects differ with age in people.

'We plan to conduct further trials soon and hope the results will help to deliver new treatments that will be of value in the fight against osteoporosis.'
August 2009

⇨ The above information is reprinted with kind permission from Arthritis Research Campaign. Visit www.arc.org.uk for more information.
© Arthritis Research Campaign

Behind the medical headlines – cannabis

Summary

Cannabis is a psychoactive drug prepared from the plant *Cannabis sativa*. Its recreational use is widespread despite being illegal in most Western countries. Concern about the psychiatric effects of cannabis use outweighs concern for the drug's physical toxicity, and largely underpins its continuing illegality, including the recent UK decision to reclassify it. In this article Drs Margot Nolan and Stephen Potts provide an informative overview of the main issues associated with cannabis use.

Key points

⇨ Cannabis is a generic term for psychoactive drugs made in various ways from plants of the Cannabis genus, mainly *Cannabis sativa*.

⇨ Psychological dependence is common.

⇨ At usual levels of intake, cannabis produces a relaxed euphoria.

⇨ Taken in excess, it can produce a variety of unpleasant symptoms, ranging from anxiety and panic attacks to disorientation and disturbed behaviour.

⇨ Prolonged use is associated with an increased risk of developing schizophrenia and other psychoses.

⇨ The physical toxicity of cannabis is primarily the toxicity of the route of delivery, and since most cannabis is smoked, concern focuses on lung cancer, respiratory disease and cardiovascular problems.

⇨ Cannabinoids have a therapeutic role, which is currently limited and requires further research.

⇨ In the UK the legal status of cannabis was downgraded from class B to class C in 2004. This decision was reversed in May 2008.

Declaration of interests: No conflict of interests declared.

Historical background

Evidence of the use of cannabis in Asia, for medicinal purposes and in religious ritual, dates back several millennia and applies across various cultures, most notably the Hindus of the Indian subcontinent. Cultivation spread gradually from Asia to Africa, Europe and the Americas, and by the late nineteenth century its therapeutic use was well established in Western culture. Legal restrictions and taxation introduced in the early twentieth century, combined with the arrival of alternative treatments, pushed cannabis use into decline until the 1960s, when recreational use spread rapidly in the West, emerging from particular subcultures to embed within the wider population.

Forms, preparations and terminology

Cannabis is a generic term for psychoactive drugs made in various ways from plants of the Cannabis genus, mainly *Cannabis sativa*. Marijuana is the herbal form, made from dried flowers and leaves, and usually consumed by rolling into a joint or reefer for smoking. Cannabis resin or hashish is a hard paste made from glandular trichomes found mainly on the flowers of female plants. It softens on heating, and is usually consumed by crumbling onto tobacco or into a water pipe to smoke. Cannabis can also be taken orally by baking it in cookies or other food, or infusing it as a tea. There is a particularly potent oil form (honey oil), made by extracting the active ingredients with a solvent, and this is usually inhaled after heating. There are many slang terms for cannabis, one of which, ganja, relates closely to ganjika, the ancient Sanskrit name for the herb.

Active ingredients

Extracts from the cannabis plant contain several hundred chemicals, many of which are psychoactive. The primary agent is delta-9-tetrahydrocannabinol, usually abbreviated to THC. Cannabis plants vary widely in their content of THC and other cannabinoids, with evidence that illicit breeding programmes have deliberately increased levels over the past 20 years from 1–3% to the 15–20% found in particularly potent forms such as 'skunk'. This, coupled with the wide range of preparations and methods of consumption, means that the effects of cannabis, both sought and undesired, vary widely.

Mode of action

Delta-9-tetrahydrocannabinol and other components act on the endogenous cannabinoid system, first identified in the human brain in the 1980s. This system is believed to have a role in the regulation of many physiological functions, including control of movement, pain modulation and perception, coordination and balance, memory and learning, and pleasure sensations. To date, two receptor types have been identified. CB1 receptors are seen in high concentrations in the basal ganglia, hippocampus and cerebellum in the brain, and dorsal primary afferent pathways in the spinal cord, where they have an important role in pain perception. CB2 receptors are found in white blood cells, and are not involved in the psychoactive effects.

Psychological effects

Acute

At usual levels of intake, the effect

produced (and sought) is a relaxed euphoria, so that users stereotypically sit around and chat companionably, often at length and with much laughter, before lapsing into sleep. Usual levels of cannabis can also alter visual perception, distort judgement of time and distance and induce carbohydrate craving.

Taken in excess in the acute phase, cannabis can produce anxiety and panic attacks, hallucinations (both visual and auditory), delusions (usually paranoid), disorientation and disturbed behaviour, although overdose is rarely directly fatal. Because the drug persists in the body, these symptoms can be prolonged for days, and occasionally weeks, after consumption of large amounts.

Chronic

Most concern about cannabis relates to the psychiatric consequences of long-term use. The key features of physical dependence (tolerance and a withdrawal syndrome) do not often arise, but psychological dependence is common. Despite the impact of the 1936 film *Reefer Madness*, there is little to support a specific 'cannabis psychosis' linked to use of the drug. However, there is accumulating evidence that prolonged use is associated with an increased risk of developing schizophrenia and other psychoses, as well as an amotivational state and depression.

The risk of psychosis appears to be greater when cannabis use is heavy, begins in early adolescence and occurs in those with a genetic vulnerability, as indicated by a family history. The risk is also greater with higher levels of THC, and in those with an established diagnosis of schizophrenia: continued cannabis use makes relapses more frequent, longer in duration and more difficult to treat, thereby worsening the outcome.

Physical effects

The toxicity of cannabis is primarily the toxicity of the route of delivery, and since most cannabis is smoked, concern focuses on lung cancer, respiratory disease and vascular diseases affecting the heart, brain and peripheries. There is conflicting evidence about the degree to which THC and other agents add to (or perhaps protect

against) the risks of smoking itself. In utero exposure has been associated with low birth weight and height, neurological abnormalities, non-lymphocytic leukaemia, behavioural disturbance and learning problems. Salmonella, fungi and infectious bacteria have been cultured from marijuana, which may pose a risk for immunosuppressed patients using it therapeutically.

Medicinal use

The list of symptoms and conditions for which there are beneficial claims for cannabis is long and varied. In recent years, legal, prescribable preparations have been industrially developed for the pharmaceutical market in a number of forms, and with a currently restricted range of indications. The best evidence for efficacy relates to nabilone, a synthetic cannabinoid analogue of THC, prescribable in the UK for chemotherapy-induced nausea if other agents prove ineffective. Sativex, a buccal spray, is a cannabis extract containing THC and cannabidiol. It has been licensed in Canada for prescription use in neuropathic pain associated with multiple sclerosis since 2005, and for pain associated with cancer since 2007. Further clinical trials are under way, and may result in approval for prescription use in these conditions in the US, the UK and mainland Europe. Dronabinol (trade name Marinol) is a preparation of THC used in the US to treat wasting and nausea in HIV/AIDS and cancer, but it is not currently licensed in the UK.

Clinical trials are investigating the use of preparations of cannabis and cannabinoids in a number of neurological conditions, such as traumatic brain injury, and in some non-neurological conditions, such as irritable bowel disease and glaucoma. More research is required to identify indications, appropriate doses and adverse effects, before the medical use of these agents will be generally accepted in the UK.

Legal status

Concern about the psychiatric consequences of cannabis use, and fears cannabis might be a 'gateway' drug to other agents such as heroin and cocaine, underpin its continued

illegality in most countries, although legalisation campaigns have been repeatedly mounted. In 'coffee shops' found – now in decreasing numbers – in parts of the Netherlands and some other Western countries, cannabis has achieved a semi-legal status, allowing consumers to purchase it without fear of arrest.

Psychological dependence on cannabis is common

In 2004 the legal status of cannabis in the UK was downgraded from class B (alongside amphetamines) to class C (alongside GHB, ketamine and diazepam). This decision was reversed in May 2008, against the recommendations of the UK Government's own advisory body. The penalty for production and trafficking is the same for both drug classes, at 14 years, while the maximum sentence for possession of a class B drug is five years, against two years for class C. In fact, while it was placed in class C, possession of cannabis was much more likely to result in a warning or caution than prosecution and imprisonment, unless there were aggravating factors. In reclassifying the drug, the Government has declared its wish for more robust enforcement of the law against supply and possession. In specific recognition of the psychiatric risks of cannabis use, new aggravating factors in sentencing will be introduced, including the supply of cannabis near mental health institutions.

Authors
⇨ Dr SG Potts, Consultant Psychiatrist, Department of Psychological Medicine, Royal Infirmary of Edinburgh, Edinburgh, UK
⇨ Dr M Nolan, Specialist Registrar in Psychiatry, Department of Psychological Medicine, Royal Infirmary of Edinburgh, Edinburgh, UK

Cannabis and mental health

Information from the Royal College of Psychiatrists

What is cannabis?

Cannabis sativa and *cannabis indica* are members of the nettle family that have grown wild throughout the world for centuries. Both plants have been used for a variety of purposes including hemp to make rope and textiles, as a medical herb and as the popular recreational drug.

The plant is used as:
⇨ the resin – a brown/black lump, known as bhang, ganja, hashish, resin, etc.
⇨ Herbal cannabis – made up of the dried flowering tops and variable amounts of dried leaves – known as grass, marijuana, spliff, weed, etc.

Skunk refers to a range of stronger types of cannabis, grown for their higher concentration of active substances. The name refers to the pungent smell they give off while growing. They can be grown either under grow-lights or in a greenhouse, often using hydroponic (growing in nutrient-rich liquids rather than soil) techniques. There are hundreds of other varieties of cannabis with exotic names such as AK-47 or Destroyer.

Street cannabis can come in a wide variety of strengths, so it is often not possible to judge exactly what is being used in any one particular session.

How is it used?

Most commonly, the resin or the dried leaves are mixed with tobacco and smoked as a 'spliff' or 'joint'. The smoke is inhaled strongly and held in the lungs for a number of seconds. It can also be smoked in a pipe, a water pipe, or collected in a container before inhaling it – a 'bucket'. It can be brewed as tea or cooked in cakes.

More than half of its psychologically active chemical ingredients are absorbed into the blood when smoked. These compounds tend to build up in fatty tissues throughout the body, so it takes a long time to be excreted in the urine. This is why cannabis can be detected in urine up to 56 days after it has last been used.

What is its legal status in the UK?

Cannabis was re-classified in January 2009 and is now a class B drug under the Misuse of Drugs Act, 1971.

The maximum penalties are:
⇨ For possession: five-year prison sentence or an unlimited fine, or both;
⇨ For dealing/supplying: 14-year prison sentence or an unlimited fine, or both.

Young people in possession of cannabis

A young person found to be in possession of cannabis will be:
⇨ Arrested;
⇨ Taken to a police station;
⇨ Given a reprimand, final warning or charge, depending on the offence.

After one reprimand, a further offence will lead to a final warning or charge.

After a final warning:
⇨ The young person must be referred to a Youth Offending Team to arrange a rehabilitation programme;
⇨ A further offence will lead to a criminal charge.

Adults in possession of cannabis

This will usually result in a warning and confiscation of the drug. Some cases may lead to arrest and either caution or prosecution, including:
⇨ repeat offending;
⇨ smoking in a public place;
⇨ threatening public order.

How does it work and what is the chemical make-up of cannabis?

There are about 400 chemical compounds in an average cannabis plant. The four main compounds are called delta-9-tetrahydrocannabinol (delta-9-THC), cannabidiol, delta-8-tetrahydrocannabinol and cannabinol. Apart from cannabidiol (CBD), these compounds are psychoactive, the strongest one being delta-9-tetrahydrocannabinol. The stronger varieties of the plant contain little cannabidiol (CBD), whilst the delta-9-THC content is a lot higher.

When cannabis is smoked, its compounds rapidly enter the bloodstream and are transported directly to the brain and other parts of the body. The feeling of being 'stoned' or 'high' is caused mainly by the delta-9-THC binding to cannabinoid receptors in the brain. A receptor is a site on a brain cell where certain substances can stick or 'bind' for a while. If this happens, it has an effect on the cell and the nerve impulses it produces. Curiously, there are also cannabis-like substances produced naturally by the brain itself – these are called endocannabinoids.

Most of these receptors are found in the parts of the brain that influence pleasure, memory, thought, concentration, sensory and time perception. Cannabis compounds can also affect the eyes, the ears, the skin and the stomach.

What are its effects?

Pleasant

A 'high' – a sense of relaxation, happiness, sleepiness, colours appear more intense, music sounds better.

Unpleasant

Around one in ten cannabis users have unpleasant experiences, including confusion, hallucinations, anxiety and paranoia. The same person may have either pleasant or unpleasant effects depending on their mood and circumstances. These feelings are usually only temporary – although as the drug can stay in the system for some weeks, the effect can be more long-lasting than users realise. Long-term use can have a depressant effect, reducing motivation.

Education and learning

There have also been suggestions that cannabis may interfere with a person's capacity to:
⇨ concentrate;
⇨ organise information;
⇨ use information.

This effect seems to last several weeks after use, which can cause particular problems for students.

However, a large study in New Zealand followed 1,265 children for 25 years. It found that cannabis use in adolescence was linked to poor school performance, but that there was no direct connection between the two. It looked as though it was simply because cannabis use encouraged a way of life that didn't help with schoolwork.

Work

It seems to have a similar effect on people at work. There is no evidence that cannabis causes specific health hazards. But users are more likely to leave work without permission, spend work time on personal matters or simply daydream. Cannabis users themselves report that drug use has interfered with their work and social life.

Of course, some areas of work are more demanding than others. A review of the research on the effect of cannabis on pilots revealed that those who had used cannabis made far more mistakes, both major and minor, than when they had not smoked cannabis. As you can imagine, the pilots were tested in flight simulators, not actually flying... The worst effects were in the first four hours, although they persisted for at least 24 hours, even when the pilot had no sense at all of being 'high'. It concluded: 'Most of us, with this evidence, would not want to fly with a pilot who had smoked cannabis within the last day or so.'

What about driving?

In New Zealand, researchers found that those who smoked regularly, and had smoked before driving, were more likely to be injured in a car crash. A recent study in France looked at over 10,000 drivers who were involved in fatal car crashes. Even when the influence of alcohol was taken into account, cannabis users were more than twice as likely to be the cause of a fatal crash than to be one of the victims. So – perhaps most of us would also not want to be driven by somebody who had smoked cannabis in the last day or so.

Mental health problems

There is growing evidence that people with serious mental illness, including depression and psychosis, are more

likely to use cannabis or have used it for long periods of time in the past. Regular use of the drug has appeared to double the risk of developing a psychotic episode or long-term schizophrenia. However, does cannabis cause depression and schizophrenia or do people with these disorders use it as a medication?

Over the past few years, research has strongly suggested that there is a clear link between early cannabis use and later mental health problems in those with a genetic vulnerability – and that there is a particular issue with the use of cannabis by adolescents.

Depression

A study following 1,600 Australian schoolchildren aged 14 to 15 for seven years found that while children who use cannabis regularly have a significantly higher risk of depression, the opposite was not the case – children who already suffered from depression were not more likely than anyone else to use cannabis. However, adolescents who used cannabis daily were five times more likely to develop depression and anxiety in later life.

Schizophrenia

Three major studies followed large numbers of people over several years, and showed that those people who use cannabis have a higher than average risk of developing schizophrenia. If you start smoking it before the age of 15, you are four times more likely to develop a psychotic disorder by the time you are 26. They found no evidence of self-medication. It seemed that, the more cannabis someone used, the more likely they were to develop symptoms.

Why should teenagers be particularly vulnerable to the use of cannabis? No one knows for certain, but it may be something to do with brain development. The brain is still developing in the teenage years – up to the age of around 20, in fact. A massive process of 'neural pruning' is going on. This is rather like streamlining a tangled jumble of circuits so they can work more effectively. Any experience, or substance, that affects this process has the potential to produce long-term psychological effects.

Recent research in Europe, and in the UK, has suggested that people who have a family background of mental

illness – and so probably have a genetic vulnerability anyway – are more likely to develop schizophrenia if they use cannabis as well.

Physical health problems

The main risk to physical health from cannabis is probably from the tobacco that it is often smoked with.

Is there such a thing as 'cannabis psychosis'?

Recent research in Denmark suggests that yes, there is. It is a short-lived psychotic disorder that seems to be brought on by cannabis use but which subsides fairly quickly once the individual has stopped using it. It's quite unusual though – in the whole of Denmark they found only around 100 new cases per year.

However, they also found that:
⇨ three-quarters had a different psychotic disorder diagnosed within the next year;
⇨ nearly half still had a psychotic disorder three years later.

So, it also seems probable that nearly half of those diagnosed as having cannabis psychosis are actually showing the first signs of a more long-lasting psychotic disorder, such as schizophrenia. It may be this group of people who are particularly vulnerable to the effects of cannabis, and so should probably avoid it in the future.

Is cannabis addictive?

It has some of the features of addictive drugs, such as:
⇨ tolerance – having to take more and more to get the same effect.
⇨ withdrawal symptoms. These have been shown in heavy users and include:
  ↳ craving;
  ↳ decreased appetite;
  ↳ sleep difficulty;
  ↳ weight loss;
  ↳ aggression and/or anger;
  ↳ irritability;
  ↳ restlessness;
  ↳ strange dreams.

These symptoms of withdrawal produce about the same amount of discomfort as withdrawing from tobacco.

For regular, long-term users:
⇨ three out of four experience cravings;

⇨ half become irritable;

⇨ seven out of ten switch to tobacco in an attempt to stay off cannabis.

The irritability, anxiety and problems with sleeping usually appear ten hours after the last joint, and peak at around one week after the last use of the drug.

Compulsive use

The user feels they have to have it and spends much of their life seeking, buying and using it. They cannot stop even when other important parts of their life (family, school, work) suffer.

You are most likely to become dependent on cannabis if you use it every day.

Dried flowers from the Cannabis sativa plant

What about skunk and other stronger varieties?

The amount of the main psycho-active ingredient, THC, that you get in herbal cannabis varies hugely from as low as 1% up to 15%. The newer strains, including skunk, can have up to 20%. The newer varieties are, on the whole, two or three times stronger than those that were available 30 years ago. It works more quickly, and can produce hallucinations with profound relaxation and elation – along with nervousness, anxiety attacks, projectile vomiting and a strong desire to eat. They may be used by some as a substitute for Ecstasy or LSD.

Legally, these strains remain classified class B drugs. While there is little research so far, it is likely that these stronger strains carry a higher risk of causing mental illness. A major study, currently underway, has already reported problems with concentration and short-term memory in users of stronger types of cannabis.

Problems with cannabis use

Many – perhaps most – people who use cannabis do enjoy it. But it can become a problem for some people. A US organisation, marijuana-anonymous.org, defines the problems of cannabis as follows:

'If cannabis controls our lives and our thinking, and if our desires centre around marijuana – scoring it, dealing it, and finding ways to stay high so that we lose interest in all else.'

The website carries the following questionnaire – which could equally well apply to alcohol use.

'If you answer "Yes" to any of the questions, you may have a problem.

1 Has smoking pot stopped being fun?

2 Do you ever get high alone?

3 Is it hard for you to imagine a life without marijuana?

4 Do you find that your friends are determined by your marijuana use?

5 Do you smoke marijuana to avoid dealing with your problems?

6 Do you smoke pot to cope with your feelings?

7 Does your marijuana use let you live in a privately defined world?

8 Have you ever failed to keep promises you made about cutting down or controlling your dope smoking?

9 Has marijuana caused problems with memory, concentration or motivation?

10 When your stash is nearly empty, do you feel anxious or worried about how to get more?

11 Do you plan your life around your marijuana use?

12 Have friends or relatives ever complained that your pot smoking is damaging your relationship with them?'

Reducing cannabis use

The Home Office recently published a guide on how to cut down and stop cannabis use. It suggests a range of things you can do to successfully stop using, including:

⇨ drawing up a list of reasons for wanting to change;

⇨ planning how you will change;

⇨ thinking about coping with withdrawal symptoms;

⇨ having a back-up plan.

www.homeoffice.gov.uk/materials/ kc-stop.pdf

If you decide to give up cannabis, it may be no more difficult than giving up cigarettes.

You could try:

⇨ to do it yourself – work through the leaflet on the FRANK website (www.talktofrank.com)

Many people will be able to stop on their own. However, if this isn't enough:

⇨ Join a support group, for instance the online www.marijuana-anonymous.org

⇨ www.connexions.gov.uk is a website for 13- to 19-year-olds which offers support and can put you in touch with a practitioner or personal adviser.

⇨ Talk to your GP or practice nurse. They will have a lot of experience in helping people to cut down their drinking and to stop smoking. They can also refer you to more specialist services, such as a counsellor, support group or NHS substance misuse service.

⇨ NHS substance misuse services offer assessment and counselling for a range of street drugs, aiming to help with:

↳ harm reduction – reducing the impact of the drug on your life;

↳ abstinence – stopping completely;

↳ relapse prevention – not starting to use again;

↳ some offer a specific service for cannabis users.

This information was produced by our Public Education Editorial Board.
Series editor: Dr Philip Timms.
Expert review: Dr Eilish Gilvarry, Dr Zerin Atakan & the Addictions Faculty.
User and Carer input: Special Committee of Patients and Carers.
With grateful thanks to Jane Feinmann.
Updated: February 2009

⇨ The above information is an extract from a leaflet published by the Royal College of Psychiatrists and is reprinted with permission. Visit www.rcpsych.ac.uk for more information or to view the full text.

Schizophrenia link to cannabis denied

A study by North Staffordshire academics has rejected a link between smoking cannabis and an increase in mental illness

The research found there were no rises in cases of schizophrenia or psychoses diagnosed in the UK over nine years, during which the use of the drug had grown substantially.

Pro-cannabis campaigners seized on the results as supporting the legalising of cannabis, and claimed the report had been suppressed.

But the leading expert behind the study said it could be too low-key to re-ignite the debate on whether restrictions should be removed from soft drugs.

From their base at the Harplands Psychiatric Hospital in Hartshill, the four experts reviewed the notes of hundreds of thousands of patients at 183 GP practices throughout the country to look for any changing rate in cases of schizophrenia.

The work had been set up to see if earlier forecasts from other experts had been borne out, that the mental disorder would soar through the growing popularity of cannabis.

Published in the *Schizophrenia Research* journal, a paper on the study said: 'A recent review concluded that cannabis use increases the risk of psychotic outcomes.

'Furthermore an accepted model of the association between cannabis and schizophrenia indicated its incidence would increase from 1990 onwards.

'We examined trends in the annual psychosis incidence and prevalence as measured by diagnosed cases from 1996 to 2005 and found it to be either stable or declining.

'The casual models linking cannabis with schizophrenia and other psychoses are therefore not supported by our study.'

The research was conducted by Drs Martin Frisher and Orsolina Martino, from the department of medicines management at Keele University;

psychiatrist Professor Ilana Crome, from the Harplands academic unit, who specialises in addiction; and diseases expert Professor Peter Croft, from the university's primary care research centre.

Its findings come shortly after the Government reclassified cannabis from class C to class B, which invokes heavier penalties.

Yet Dr Frisher revealed last night that the study had been partly commissioned by the Government's Advisory Committee on the Misuse of Drugs.

The research found there were no rises in cases of schizophrenia or psychoses diagnosed in the UK over nine years, during which the use of the drug had grown substantially

---

He said: 'We concentrated on looking into the incidence of schizophrenia during those years and not specifically at cannabis use.

'It was relatively low-key research so I don't believe it will re-ignite the debate on whether the drug should be legalised.'

Hartshill-based Dilys Wood, national co-ordinator of the Legalise Cannabis Alliance, said that so far the report had been published in medical journals and would have a far-reaching reaction if it surfaced more widely.

She added: 'I believe that if it had found a causal link between cannabis and schizophrenia it would have been all over the press.

'The public needs to know the truth about drugs; not more Government-led propaganda.'

And Alliance press officer Don Barnard said: 'It is hard to believe the then Home Secretary Jacqui Smith did not know of this very important research when deciding to upgrade cannabis to class B.'

The team said a number of alternative explanations for the stabilising of schizophrenia had been considered and while they could not be wholly discounted, they did not appear to be plausible.
27 August 2009

⇨ The above information is reprinted with kind permission from Staffordshire Sentinel News & Media Ltd. Visit www.thisisstaffordshire.co.uk for more information.

Skunk 'poses greatest risk of psychosis'

Information from the Institute of Psychiatry, King's College London

Researchers at the Institute of Psychiatry at King's College London (KCL) have found that people who smoke skunk, the most potent form of cannabis available in the UK, are almost seven times more likely to develop psychotic illnesses than those who use traditional cannabis resin (hash) or grass.

The study, funded by the Maudsley Charitable Fund and the National Institute for Health Research specialist Biomedical Research Centre for Mental Health at South London and Maudsley NHS Foundation Trust (SLaM) and KCL, is published today in the *British Journal of Psychiatry*.

The team collected information on cannabis use from 280 people attending SLaM with their first episode of psychosis. A control group of 174 healthy people from the local area was also studied. There was no significant difference between the two groups in whether they had ever used cannabis or their age at first use; however, the patients with psychosis were twice as likely to have used cannabis for longer than five years, and over six times more likely to use it every day. Among those who had used cannabis, patients with psychosis were almost seven times more likely to use skunk than the control subjects.

Psychiatrist and lead researcher Dr Marta Di Forti said: 'In both groups a high proportion had used cannabis at some point in their lives and they were both likely to have started early in adolescence; however, psychosis was associated with more frequent and longer use. Our most striking finding was that among those who had used cannabis and developed psychosis, the type of cannabis which was preferentially used was the high-potency skunk variety.'

The researchers believe the high level of delta-9 tetrahydrocannabinol (Δ9-THC) found in skunk is to blame.

The two main constituents of cannabis are Δ9-THC and cannabidiol. Δ9-THC is the main psychoactive ingredient, and in experiments has been shown to produce psychotic symptoms such as hallucinations and delusions. Cannabidiol does not induce these symptoms and seems to have anti-psychotic properties – possibly counteracting the effects of THC.

People who smoke skunk, the most potent form of cannabis available in the UK, are almost seven times more likely to develop psychotic illnesses than those who use traditional cannabis resin (hash) or grass

---

In south-east London, where the study was carried out, the skunk variety of cannabis contains 12–18% Δ9-THC and less than 1.5% cannabidiol. In contrast, resin (hash), which was preferred by cannabis users in the study's control group, has an average Δ9-THC of 3.4% and a similar proportion of cannabidiol.

Dr Di Forti concluded: 'Our study is the first to demonstrate that the risk of psychosis is much greater among people who are frequent cannabis users, especially among those using skunk, rather than among occasional users of traditional hash. It is not surprising that those who use skunk daily have the highest risk of all, because skunk has the highest concentration of Δ9-THC and a relative lack of cannabidiol with its protective effect.'

She added: 'Unfortunately, skunk is displacing traditional cannabis preparations in many countries, and the availability of skunk on the UK 'street' market has steadily increased over the past six years. Public education about the risks of heavy use of high-potency cannabis is vital.'
A copy of the paper can be accessed: http://bjp.rcpsych.org/cgi/content/abstract/195/6/488
1 December 2009

⇨ The above information is reprinted with kind permission from the Institute of Psychiatry, King's College London. Visit www.iop.kcl.ac.uk for more information.

© *Institute of Psychiatry, King's College London*

'Cannabis alters DNA'

Research at University of Leicester highlights cancer risk from cannabis smoke

A new study published by University of Leicester researchers has found 'convincing evidence' that cannabis smoke damages DNA in ways that could potentially increase the risk of cancer development in humans.

Using a newly developed highly sensitive liquid chromatography-tandem mass spectrometry method, the University of Leicester scientists found clear indication that cannabis smoke damages DNA, under laboratory conditions.

They have now published the findings in the journal *Chemical Research in Toxicology*[1].

A new study published has found 'convincing evidence' that cannabis smoke damages DNA in ways that could potentially increase the risk of cancer

The research was carried out by Rajinder Singh, Jatinderpal Sandhu, Balvinder Kaur, Tina Juren, William P. Steward, Dan Segerback and Peter B. Farmer from the Cancer Biomarkers and Prevention Group, Department of Cancer Studies and Molecular Medicine and Karolinska Institute, Sweden.

Raj Singh said: 'Parts of the plant *Cannabis sativa*, also known as marijuana, ganja, and various street names, are commonly smoked as a recreational drug, although its use for such purposes is illegal in many countries.

'There have been many studies on the toxicity of tobacco smoke. It is known that tobacco smoke contains 4,000 chemicals of which 60 are classed as carcinogens. Cannabis in contrast has not been so well studied. It is less combustible than tobacco and is often mixed with tobacco in use. Cannabis smoke contains 400 compounds including 60 cannabinoids. However, because of its lower combustibility it contains 50% more carcinogenic polycyclic aromatic hydrocarbons including naphthalene, benzanthracene and benzopyrene, than tobacco smoke.'

Writing in the journal *Chemical Research in Toxicology*, the scientists describe the development of a mass spectrometry method that provides a clear indication that cannabis smoke damages DNA, under laboratory conditions.

The authors added: 'It is well known that toxic substances in tobacco smoke can damage DNA and increase the risk of lung and other cancers. Scientists were unsure though whether cannabis smoke would have the same effect. Our research has focused on the toxicity of acetaldehyde, which is present in both tobacco and cannabis.'

The researchers add that the ability of cannabis smoke to damage DNA has significant human health implications, especially as users tend to inhale more deeply than cigarette smokers, which increases respiratory burden. 'The smoking of three to four cannabis cigarettes a day is associated with the same degree of damage to bronchial mucus membranes as 20 or more tobacco cigarettes a day,' the team adds.

'These results provide evidence for the DNA-damaging potential of cannabis smoke,' the researchers conclude, 'implying that the consumption of cannabis cigarettes may be detrimental to human health with the possibility to initiate cancer development.'

The study was funded by the European Union Network of Excellence ECNIS, the Medical Research Council and Cancer Research UK.

Note

1 Rajinder Singh, Jatinderpal Sandhu, Balvinder Kaur, Tina Juren, William P. Steward, Dan Segerback and Peter B. Farmer (2009) Evaluation of the DNA Damaging Potential of Cannabis Cigarette Smoke by the Determination of Acetaldehyde Derived N^2-Ethyl-2'-deoxyguanosine Adducts. *Chemical Research in Toxicology*, 22, 1181–1188.

16 June 2009

⇨ The above information is reprinted with kind permission from the University of Leicester. Visit www.le.ac.uk for more information.

Cannabis and your health

The debate on cannabis and its impact on health has been simmering for decades, and although various physical and mental effects have been associated with using the drug, only a handful of these claims has proved conclusive. TheSite.org weighs up the evidence

In the first half of the 20th century, legal issues led to a great deal of propaganda. Cannabis had been made illegal in 1928 and opponents of the drug wanted people to know about its dangers. A famous piece of propaganda was the film *Reefer Madness*. The film follows a group of high-school students whose marijuana misuse leads to catastrophic consequences, such as manslaughter, rape and suicide. As the medical community learnt more about cannabis, more varied reports started to hit the headlines. Today, conflicting medical research continues to further baffle the situation. So what are the health implications of taking cannabis?

Short-term health effects

Cannabis affects different people in different ways depending on a number of factors. These include how much you take, what type of cannabis you take, how experienced you are in using the drug, and your own mental state. The immediate effects of cannabis are short term and can be identified easily:

⇨ The good – users will normally experience a period of euphoric intoxication commonly called a 'high'. This is the desired outcome for most people who take the drug;

⇨ The bad – many will suffer from short-term memory loss and will have a reduced attention span after taking cannabis;

⇨ The ugly – the more undesired psychological effects of taking the drug can sometimes overwhelm smokers. Increased anxiety, paranoia and panic attacks are some of the unwanted effects you may experience (this state is sometimes called a 'whitey', because the person's face will turn a ghostly pale colour).

Some people who take the drug have also reported being affected by longer-lasting psychological episodes involving hallucinations and delusions.

Long-term health effects

The longer-term health effects of cannabis are harder to confirm because the drug is often taken in conjunction with other drugs such as alcohol and tobacco.

Lung cancer

The alleged link between smoking cannabis and lung cancer has spawned a big debate in the medical world. Despite several reports, there has been no overwhelming proof of this link and a general conclusion has yet to be reached.

The main problem is the fact that most people who smoke cannabis do so in conjunction with tobacco, which is known to be carcinogenic. Cannabis smokers also hold the smoke in their lungs for much longer to obtain the maximum hit from the smoke, which could put them at greater risk to any pollutants in the smoke.

A 2007 study by researchers at the Medical Research institute of New Zealand found that a single cannabis joint may cause as much damage to the lungs as five cigarettes. The research involved a group of 339 volunteers aged 18 to 70 who were divided into four groups according to whether they smoked only cannabis, only tobacco, both, or were non-smokers. Each volunteer had lung function tests and X-ray scans of their chests to assess the level of damage to their lungs and airways.

A conflicting study published in 2006 by the University of California concluded that there was no link between smoking cannabis and lung cancer. A total of 611 lung cancer patients living in Los Angeles and 601 patients with other cancers of the head and neck were compared with 1,040 people without cancer. All the participants were asked about their use of marijuana, tobacco and alcohol, as well as other drugs, their

I'M DOING A HEALTH RESEARCH PROJECT

diets, occupation, and their family history of lung cancer.

Cannabis and mental health

Cannabis use is often linked with the development of psychotic illnesses in later life. In July 2007 researchers from Bristol and Cardiff universities published research that claimed cannabis users are 40% more likely to suffer a psychotic illness than non-users. Critics of this research argue that if cannabis does cause mental illnesses then the number of people with mental health conditions would have increased dramatically over the past 30 years, whereas the proportion of people with schizophrenia has remained roughly the same.

Fertility

Research into the effects of cannabis on fertility has also proved inconclusive. Tests on animals have shown that high doses of THC (the main psychoactive substance found in cannabis) lowers testosterone, impairs sperm production, and disrupts the ovulation cycle. However, there are contradictory reports which claim that fertility rates are not affected by cannabis use.

Cancer healing claims

Research by Harvard University suggests that THC may have cancer healing potential. In lab and mouse studies, THC cut lung tumour growth in half and helped prevent the cancer from spreading.

Cannabis for pain relief

Cannabis has been used for centuries for medicinal purposes. It has even been claimed that Queen Victoria was prescribed the drug to relieve period pain. A report by the House of Lords Science and Technology Committee found that cannabis was being used in Britain by people with multiple sclerosis, epilepsy and ME as a method of pain relief.

Doctors in Britain are allowed to prescribe Nabilone (capsules containing THC) to patients suffering from nausea caused by chemotherapy. However, patients who take the drug in capsule form complain that they cannot control the amount that they take, which causes the undesired side effects of cannabis. Pharmaceutical companies have started developing THC aerosols and inhalers that don't damage the lungs. This would enable patients to control the amount of THC they take and reduce the side effects. *Written by Chris Denholm*

⇨ The above information is reprinted with kind permission from TheSite. org. Visit www.thesite.org for more.

© *TheSite.org*

Medicinal use of cannabis

Information from politics.co.uk

What is cannabis?

Cannabis is a durable hemp plant. The cannabis plant can be used to produce a number of products including seeds, pulp and medicine. The pulp is used as fuel and to make paper, the seed is used in foods, and the oil from the seed can be used as a base for paints and varnishes. The blossoms and leaves of the hemp plant produce a sticky resin, which has historically been used in a variety of medicinal functions, and for just as long, for recreational drug use.

The compound which gives cannabis its depressant and mood-altering properties is known as THC.

Some people believe that cannabis has positive therapeutic qualities and is felt to be particularly useful for certain conditions, such as multiple sclerosis.

Background

In the early 1900s cannabis was popular both as a recreational and a medicinal compound, and there are suggestions that Queen Victoria was given cannabis by her doctor to relieve period pain. The development of superior alternatives, such as the invention of the syringe for rapid drug inducement and the development of aspirin, alongside the failure to develop a standardised product and the poor rate of absorption from oral inhalation, led to the reduced use of cannabis in medicine.

Cannabis was first made illegal in the UK in 1928, and medical use was outlawed in 1973. However, during the 1980s and 1990s, cannabis was increasingly used as a recreational drug, and medical interest in cannabis and its derivatives (cannabinoids) began to grow, principally on the strength of anecdotal evidence from illegal self-medication.

A number of reports about cannabis were published during the late 1990s: by the British Medical Association (1997), the US National Institutes of Health and the American Medical Association (1997), the Department of Health (1998) and the House of Lords Science and Technology Select Committee (1998).

The Select Committee report found cannabis was being used by people with multiple sclerosis, epilepsy, ME and other pain, and as an anti-emetic after chemotherapy, and claimed that this is 'sometimes connived at by the medical professions'.

The report recommended allowing the use of cannabis in some circumstances, but the proposals were rejected by the Government. Although policy remained unchanged, a 2001 follow-up report suggested that the Government's attitude was changing, stating: 'the Minister assured us that once a safe, effective, cannabis-

based medicine had been licensed by the Medicines Control Agency, the Government would actively co-operate in permitting it to be prescribed'.

In 2002, Home Secretary David Blunkett announced that he might permit the medical use of cannabis if clinical trials of the drug were successful.

September 2003 saw the Netherlands become the first country in the world to explicitly legalise the use of cannabis for medical purposes and to licence its production and sale through pharmacies. In the US, the Food and Drug Administration has approved the oral use of dronabinol, a cannabis derivative, for people with AIDS, as a means of restoring appetite.

In January 2004, the Home Office downgraded cannabis from a class B to a class C drug for all purposes, but this decision was reversed in May 2008 by Home Secretary Jacqui Smith who announced that cannabis was to be reclassified as a class B drug.

It remains illegal to carry, smoke or possess cannabis in any form, but the police usually won't arrest or prosecute people found in possession of small amounts intended for personal use.

Controversies

Despite its potential medical value, cannabis has long been thought to have harmful mental health side-effects, with many scientific reports linking it to depression, schizophrenia and other conditions.

There have been a number of high-profile prosecutions of medicinal cannabis users in the UK, and the Science and Technology Committee report warned of regional variations in the verdicts and sentences handed down, or 'postcode prosecuting'. Figures and trends have been difficult to extrapolate, however, as the Home Office does not record instances in which therapeutic use is pleaded in mitigation.

Therapeutic use prosecutions are particularly controversial given the seriousness of some of the conditions of the users, including cancer, AIDS and MS, which has generated public sympathy for a change in the law.

However, the large quantities, steady supplies and high quality of the product required by medicinal users has tended to make their cases more difficult for the authorities to ignore than casual users.

Medicinal use is one of the leading positive factors cited by those calling for legalisation of cannabis. Indeed, a synthetic form of THC – Nabilone – has been licensed for use as an anti-emetic in prescription drugs since 1982. The drugs industry has also been developing aerosol sprays for delivering THC directly to the lungs without the health risks of smoking.

The criminalisation of those using cannabis for medicinal purposes has been a particularly controversial issue, with opponents questioning the social purpose and moral value of the law that punishes individuals merely for seeking an effective form of pain relief not available from conventional, legal sources.

Quotes

'Thousands of people do treat themselves medically with cannabis. They spend excessive amounts of time and money in order to get their supply, without any guarantee of its strength, quality or purity. They risk confiscation, fines, criminal records and imprisonment. Why would they do this if cannabis was not an effective medication – indeed so effective it is worth risking everything rather than use a medication that the authorities have deemed "legal"?'
UKCIA – 2008

'Drugs legislation intends to protect us from harmful drugs; I absolutely agree with that aim, but the present policy is a disaster. It is hardly in the public interest to prosecute a disabled man for mitigating his symptoms. I smoke for my health, not to jeopardise it.'
Disabled Londoner Edwin Stratton, challenging his prosecution for growing cannabis to treat pain and nausea caused by coeliac disease – October 2008

'It has been discovered that long-term cannabis smokers may suffer a dramatic and obvious form of premature brain atrophy (brain shrinkage). This has become apparent

Statistics

A recent Home Office study revealed that herbal cannabis accounted for 81% of all cannabis seized by the police on the street when giving a warning to users. Significantly 97% of the herbal was sinsemilla or 'skunk'.

Cannabis resin used to be much more popular (70% in 2002) than herbal cannabis.

Since 1990, when intensively-grown cannabis, sinsemilla or 'skunk' first appeared in the UK its potency has slowly increased and the mean is now 16.2%.
Source: Home Office Cannabis Potency Study – May 2008
Sativex, a cannabis-based medicine, is currently taken as an oral spray by around 1,200 people with MS in the UK.
Source: MS Society – 2008

by brain-scan studies of the brains of habitual cannabis-users. It seems therefore grossly inappropriate that we should treat one established form of brain damage, due to the MS, with a method which results in even more extensive, and permanent, brain damage, due to the cannabis.'
Dr M R Lawrence, MS Resource Centre – 2008

⇨ The above information is reprinted with kind permission from politics. co.uk. Visit www.politics.co.uk for more information.

© Adfero

Marijuana use around the world

The Global Cannabis Commission Report

Introduction – cannabis as an issue

Marijuana is the most widely used illegal drug in the world.

The United Nations Office of Drugs and Crime (UNODC) estimates that, across all nations, 160 million people used cannabis in the course of 2005, 4% of the global adult populations – far more than the number that used any other illicit drug, though far less than the number that consumed alcohol or tobacco.

The number of cannabis users in 2005 was 10% higher than estimated global use in the mid-1990s (UNODC, 2007).

The numbers are particularly striking because 50 years ago cannabis was a very uncommon drug, with pockets of traditional use in India, Jamaica and a few other developing nations and use otherwise largely confined to fringe bohemian groups in a few rich countries.

All nations prohibit both the production and use of cannabis and have been committed to do so at least since the 1961 Single Convention on Drugs.

The spread of cannabis use among adolescents and young adults led to a strong reaction in much of the developed world, which still results in large rates per capita of arrests for cannabis possession and use in nations such as Switzerland, Australia and the US.

The emergence of a new stream of research findings documenting that cannabis can trigger adverse mental health consequences for some users has recently increased popular concern.

On the other side of the policy debate there is a concern, dating back to the 1970s, that the state is intruding too much into personal life in its efforts to control cannabis use, and that criminal penalties are not justified for an offence that risks harm largely only to the user.

There has been a long-term trend towards less punitive policies in such countries as Australia, Great Britain, the Netherlands and France, although actual patterns of policing have often undermined the trend.

Now the direction of trends is less clear, in part influenced by new evidence on cannabis and mental disorders.

Using cannabis: who, where, why?

Cannabis, like other psychoactive substances such as alcohol, tobacco and opiates, is used for a variety of reasons.

For some users it is simply the pleasure of an altered state and a social experience. For others, it is a way of coping with the troubles of everyday life, a source of solace or, indeed, a source of cognitive benefits and enhanced creativity (Iversen, 2008).

For yet other users it has a therapeutic value for some physical or mental health problem. Though the medical value of cannabis is not well researched, it is plausible that it does in fact provide relief for a number of conditions, such as AIDS wasting syndrome or glaucoma (Institute of Medicine, 1999).

Cannabis first became popular in the West in the 1960s, when its use emerged as part of the general youth rebellion of that decade.

From North America it spread, over the next 20 years, to most of Western Europe, as well as to Australia. After the collapse of the Soviet Union, it also spread in the 1990s to many countries in Eastern Europe.

There is, however, substantial variation in rates of use across these nations: Finland and Sweden, for example, have rates of users on a lifetime basis that are about two-fifths the rate in Great Britain (EMCDDA, 2007: Table GPS-8).

In the countries with high rates of cannabis use, roughly half of all adults born since 1960 have used the drug. Cannabis is now used in every region of the world. The percentage of adults who report use in the past year was higher than the global average in Oceania (16%), North America (11%), Africa (8%) and Western Europe (7%). It was at or below the global average in Eastern Europe (4%), South America (2%), South-East Europe (2%) and Asia (2%) (UNODC, 2007).

Because of their larger populations, Asia and Africa accounted for 31% and 24% of global cannabis use, respectively, followed by the Americas

(24%), Europe (19%) and Oceania (2%).

The US and Australia have conducted surveys of drug use since the mid-1970s and mid-1980s respectively (AIHW, 2007; SAMHSA, 2006).

In the US in 2005, 40% of the adult population reported trying cannabis at some time in their lives, with 13% of adolescents reporting use in the past year (SAMHSA, 2006).

In Australia in 2007, 34% of persons over the age of 15 reported that they had used cannabis at some time in their lives (AIHW, 2008).

Rates are highest among youth, particularly young adults, and use tails off slowly in the mid-30s. At the other end of the age of use spectrum, the age of first use has fallen since about 2000 in some countries, but not others (Hibell et al., 2004; Degenhardt et al., 2000).

Cannabis use in the USA typically begins in the mid to late teens, and is most prevalent in the early 20s (Bachman et al., 1997). Most cannabis use is intermittent and time-limited, with very few users engaging in daily cannabis use over a period of years (Bachman et al., 1997).

In the US and Australia, about 10% of those who ever use cannabis become daily users, and another 20% to 30% use weekly (Hall & Pacula, 2003).

Cannabis use declines from the early and mid-20s to the early 30s, reflecting major role transitions in early adulthood (e.g. entering tertiary education, entering full-time employment, marrying, and having children) (Anthony, 2006; Bachman et al., 1997).

The largest decreases are seen in cannabis use among males and females after marriage, and especially after childbirth (Bachman et al., 1997; Chen & Kandel, 1995).

While marijuana use, once it is established in a society, seems never to fall to very low rates, there has been substantial variation in prevalence over the last decades.

For example, whereas in 1979 50.8% of American high-school seniors had used marijuana in the previous 12 months, by 1992 that figure had fallen to 21.9%; it then rose again to 37.8% in 1999 (Johnston et al. 2007).

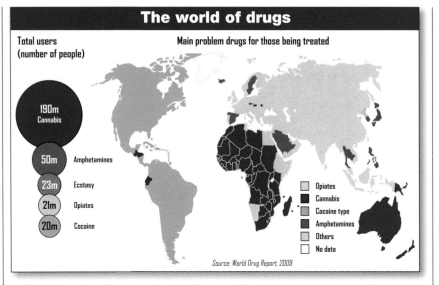

The world of drugs

Total users (number of people)

190m Cannabis
50m Amphetamines
23m Ecstasy
21m Opiates
20m Cocaine

Main problem drugs for those being treated

- Opiates
- Cannabis
- Cocaine type
- Amphetamines
- Others
- No data

Source: World Drug Report, 2009

Interestingly, there seems to be a common pattern over time across countries. For most Western nations between 1991 and 1998 there was an increase of about half in the proportion of 18-year-olds reporting that they had tried cannabis.

Since 1998 in the same countries there has been a substantial decline in that figure, though in 2006 it still remains well above the 1991 level.

The common patterns across countries with very different policy approaches reinforce the general impression that penalties for personal use have very little impact on the prevalence of cannabis use in a society.

What does explain the changes remains essentially a mystery, but popular youth culture, including representation of the drug in music, films and magazines, probably plays an important role.

The linked patterns of fluctuation in use in different countries suggest the influence across borders of a global youth popular culture.

Marijuana use can be thought of as a 'career'. Most users try the drug a few times, and are at very low risk of suffering or causing any substantial harm.

However, recent research has confirmed that a substantial fraction will use the drug regularly over the course of ten or more years, and that perhaps 10% of those trying cannabis at some stage will become dependent upon it.

Among those who begin to use in their early teens, the risk of developing problem use may be as high as one in six (Anthony, 2006).

It is worth comparing the drug's use in these respects to alcohol and tobacco on the one hand, and to cocaine and heroin on the other.

Cannabis is most like alcohol, in that most users do not become dependent but many do have using careers that stretch over years, although in current circumstances not for as long as for alcohol.

Excerpted from longer PDF document: The Global Cannabis Commission Report
1 May 2009

⇨ The above information is an extract from the Global Cannabis Commission Report and is reprinted with kind permission from the Beckley Foundation. Visit www.beckleyfoundation.org for more information or to view references for this article.

© *Beckley Foundation*

The world drugs problem, ten years on

Today the European Commission launched a report on the world's illicit drugs markets since 1998. It shows that in the past decade drug policies across the world have developed, especially at national level, as efforts to help drug users have been stepped up and tougher policies adopted against drug traffickers. But what is the result of all this on the ground?

The study on which the report is based has found no evidence that the global drug problem has been reduced during the period from 1998 to 2007. Broadly speaking the situation has improved a little in some of the richer countries, while for others it worsened, and for some of those it worsened 'sharply and substantially', among which are a few large developing or transitional countries.

In other words, the world drugs problem seems to be more or less in the same state as in 1998. If anything, the situation has become more complex. Prices for drugs in most Western countries have fallen since 1998 by as much as 10% to 30%, despite tougher sentencing of the sellers of e.g. cocaine and heroin in some of these markets. At the same time, there is no evidence that drugs have become more difficult to obtain. Cannabis use has become a 'normal' part of young people's lives in many Western countries: up to 50% of people born after 1980 have at least tried it. The majority of them, however, do not continue to use it beyond early adulthood. The study has also found that specific policies against drug production can affect the areas where drugs are produced. For example, in the past decade a part of cocaine production shifted from Peru and Bolivia to Colombia.

The publication of the report coincides with the high-level meeting that takes place in Vienna this week as part of the annual session of the UN Commission on Narcotic Drugs (CND). Ministers from around the world will finalise a period of reflection on the assessment of the implementation of the Political Declaration on the world drug problem adopted by the 20th United Nations General Assembly Special Session (UNGASS) on drugs in 1998 (a declaration aimed to significantly reduce the global illicit drugs problem by 2008 through international cooperation and measures in the field of drug supply and drug demand reduction.) This week, a new political declaration for the period 2009–19 is scheduled to be adopted on the basis of that assessment.

Vice-President Jacques Barrot, commissioner responsible for justice, freedom and security, declared: 'We cannot limit ourselves in Vienna this week to quantifying objectives. We must now seek to tackle the world drug phenomenon, based on factual evidence.'

The study seeks to provide realistic estimates of the total size of the illicit drugs market in terms of annual revenues generated. The result shows that such overall estimates are very difficult to make, mostly due to a lack of reliable data on production, consumption and trade of drugs in much of the world. Nevertheless, the study has developed estimates, for instance for the markets for cannabis, cocaine and heroin for Western Europe, the US and Oceania. The best estimate (2005) for total revenue in these three regions for cannabis is almost €70 billion, which is about half the UNODC estimate of approximately €125 billion.

An important finding is the fact that harm reduction policies, still controversial in some countries, are gaining ground in a growing number of other countries which see them as an effective way of reducing drug-related disease, social disorder and mortality.

The report also provides insights into the economic fundamentals of the global illicit drugs market, with estimates of production costs and value added throughout the trafficking chain from initial production to final retail sale. The distribution of

income among those involved in the drug trade is analysed and reveals a surprisingly mundane picture, with only a relatively small minority believed to be making significant amounts of money.

Finally, a key finding of the study is that it shows the weaknesses of the international system for the collection of data and information on the world's drug problem. Where the EU has invested large amounts of money in the further development of its drug monitoring activities through the European Monitoring Centre for Drugs and Drug Addiction (EMCDDA), such information mechanisms are not realistically within reach at world level.

Cannabis use has become a 'normal' part of young people's lives in many Western countries

---

The report of the study will be made available to the participants in the CND High Level Meeting and will be presented on Tuesday 10 March at 2pm, by Mr Lars-Erik Lundin (EU Head of Delegation in Vienna) and Carel Edwards (Head of the Anti-Drugs Policy Unit, DG JLS), during a press conference in the EU Delegation in Vienna located in Argentinierstrasse 26/corner Taubstummengasse, Meeting Room Mezzanine, A-1040 Vienna (Metro U1, exit Taubstummengasse). Contact point: Anne-Marie Huber +43.1.51618329 or + 43.699.1966579.

The study was produced by the Trimbos Institute and RAND for the European Commission's Directorate-General for Justice, Liberty and Security department. The report can be found at: http://ec.europa.eu/justice_home/ doc_centre/drugs/studies/doc_drugs_ studies_en.htm. 10 March 2009

⇨ The above information is reprinted with kind permission from the European Union. Visit http:// europa.eu for more information.

© *European Union*

Home Office cannabis potency study 2008

Executive summary. By Sheila Hardwick and Leslie King

⇨ This study was funded by the Home Office. It arose from a recommendation in the 2006 cannabis report of the Advisory Council on the Misuse of Drugs (ACMD).

⇨ The proportion of herbal cannabis has increased markedly in recent years. In 2002 it was estimated that it represented around 30% of police seizures of cannabis, but by 2004/05 had reached 55%.

⇨ 23 police forces in England and Wales participated in the study. Forces were requested to submit samples confiscated from street-level users. In early 2008, they submitted 2,921 samples for analysis to either the Forensic Science Service Ltd (FSS) or LGC Forensics at Culham (LGC F).

⇨ Initial laboratory examination showed that 80.8% were herbal cannabis and 15.3% were cannabis resin. The remaining 3.9% were either indeterminate or not cannabis.

⇨ Microscopic examination of around two-thirds of the samples showed that over 97% of the herbal cannabis had been grown by intensive methods (sinsemilla). The remainder was classed as traditional imported herbal cannabis.

⇨ Regional variations were found in the market share of herbal cannabis. Thus North Wales, South Wales, Cleveland and Devon and Cornwall submitted proportionately fewer herbal cannabis samples, whereas Essex, Metropolitan and Avon and Somerset submitted proportionately more. These differences were statistically significant at the 0.1% confidence interval.

⇨ The mean THC concentration (potency) of the sinsemilla samples was 16.2% (range = 4.1 to 46%). The median potency was 15.0%, close to values reported by others in the past few years.

⇨ The mean THC concentration (potency) of the traditional imported herbal cannabis samples was 8.4% (range = 0.3 to 22%); median = 9.0%. Only a very small number of samples were received and analysed.

⇨ The mean potency of cannabis resin was 5.9% (range = 1.3 to 27.8%). The median = 5.0% was typical of values reported by others over many years.

⇨ Cannabis resin had a mean CBD content of 3.5% (range = 0.1 to 7.3%), but the CBD content of herbal cannabis was less than 0.1% in nearly all cases.

⇨ There was a weak, but statistically significant, correlation ($r = 0.48$; $N = 112$; $P < 0.001$) between the THC and the CBD content of resin.

⇨ The above information is reprinted with kind permission from the Home Office Scientific Development Branch. Visit http://scienceandresearch. homeoffice.gov.uk for more information.

© *Crown copyright*

Why does cannabis potency matter?

World Drug Report 2009

Of the many people worldwide who use cannabis, also known as marijuana, very few understand the increase in its potency over the years. Cannabis has changed dramatically since the 1970s. New methods of production such as hydroponic cultivation have increased the potency and the negative effects of tetrahydrocannabinol (THC), the most psychoactive of the chemical substances found in marijuana. It is important to understand cannabis potency because of its link to health problems, including mental health.

The amount of THC present in a cannabis sample is generally used as a measure of cannabis potency. One of the most comprehensive studies, conducted by the European Monitoring Centre for Drugs and Drug Addiction (EMCDDA) in 2004, concluded that a modest increase in aggregate cannabis potency had occurred, possibly attributable to the use of intensive indoor cultivation methods. The authors of the study noted that, nonetheless, THC content varied widely.

While a United Kingdom Home Office study in 2008 found little change in cannabis potency: samples of sinsemilla cannabis from 2008 had a median potency of 15 per cent, compared with 14 per cent for samples from 2004/05. Long-term increases have been reported in the US, with an average potency of ten per cent reported in 2008.

There are several methodological factors that influence the ability to generate comparable data and infer trends with respect to cannabis potency. Important variables to be considered include the phytochemistry, the type of cannabis product, cultivation method, sampling and stability.

As detailed below, each of these factors can affect the measurement of cannabis potency.

Plant part used: The secretion of THC is most abundant in the flowering heads and surrounding leaves of the cannabis plant. The amount of resin secreted is influenced by environmental conditions during growth (light, temperature and humidity), sex of the plant and time of harvest. The THC content varies in the different parts of the plant: from ten to 12 per cent in flowers, one to two per cent in leaves, 0.1–0.3 per cent in stalks, to less than 0.03 per cent in the roots.

Cannabis has changed dramatically since the 1970s

Product type: There are three main types of cannabis products: herb (marijuana), resin (hashish) and oil (hash oil). Cannabis herb comprises the dried and crushed flower heads and surrounding leaves. It often contains up to five per cent THC content. However, sinsemilla, derived from the unfertilised female plant, can be much more potent. Cannabis resin can contain up to 20 per cent THC content.

The most potent form of cannabis is cannabis oil, derived from the concentrated resin extract. It may contain more than 60 per cent THC content. The increase in market share of a particular product type can influence the reported average potency values. For example, the rise to an average ten per cent CH content in samples seized in 2008 as reported by the United States Office of National Drug Control Policy is attributed to the fact that high-potency cannabis (presumably indoor-grown) has gained a 40-per-cent share of the market.

Cultivation methods: The cannabis plant grows in a variety of climates. The amount and quality of the resin produced depends on the temperature, humidity, light and soil acidity/alkalinity. Accordingly, herbal cannabis grown outdoors varies considerably in potency. Intensive indoor cultivation of female plants and clones, grown under artificial light, often without soil (using hydroponic cultivation) and with optimised cultivation conditions, produces cannabis of a consistently higher potency.

Sampling: Most data on cannabis potency are derived from the analysis of seized samples. This means that those samples must be representative of the entire seizure so that inferences and extrapolations can be made.

Stability: THC is converted to cannabinol on exposure to air and light. This process reduces the THC concentration, especially in old samples which have not been stored under suitable conditions (that is, a cool, dark place). It is believed that claimed increases in the potency of cannabis preparations confiscated in the US over a period of 18 years may not adequately take into account the issue of the stability of THC in older samples.

Only through careful examination of these factors can we make a more systematic, scientific and comparable assessment of cannabis potency in different places and over time.
29 June 2009

⇨ The above information is reprinted with kind permission from the United Nations Office on Drugs and Crime. Visit www.unodc.org for more information.
© United Nations Office on Drugs and Crime

The families torn apart by teenage skunk epidemic

It is the end of a taboo: articulate, middle-class parents are speaking out about the nightmare of seeing their children spiral into drug abuse and, all too often, mental illness. Many blame themselves for staying silent, assuming that modern strains of cannabis were little different from the pot that baby boomers smoked at college. The reality is very different

By Tracy McVeigh, chief reporter

In the front room of a stucco-fronted three-bedroom home in Chiswick, a deeply middle-class suburb in comfortable West London, Susanne apologises for the smell of the recently walked dog, but it is the sweetly oppressive stink of skunk cannabis that lingers most strongly among the plumped-up Ikea cushions.

'It does reek,' said the 52-year-old mother-of-two, sniffing. 'That bloody boy has been smoking that stuff down here when I've been out with the bloody dog.' She puts her head in her hands. 'The smell gives me such a headache.'

John and Susanne were happy to talk about life with a son who regularly uses cannabis, but changed their minds about giving their real names or occupations after watching the fallout that has engulfed author Julie Myerson, whose estrangement from her cannabis-smoking son Jake was deepened when she wrote a book about his behaviour that culminated in him being thrown out of the family home.

The couple's own 17-year-old son, also called Jake, insists on the use of his name. 'I'm not ashamed, you know. I have looked it all up and read a lot of research and I am quite well informed,' he said. 'Actually, all my friends are; it's the so-called adults who have forgotten that they did a bit of this themselves when they were young – a long time ago,' he added with a sarcastic grin at his mother.

'He reads what he wants to read, hippy websites mostly,' said his mother, who has a whole folder of clipped-out newspaper articles and Internet printouts full of research and opinion on cannabis that she

regularly tries to get Jake to read. It sounds like a well-rehearsed exchange between the pair.

'We certainly have had these discussions again and again for two years. Paradoxically, it's when he's stoned that he actually engages,' she said.

His parents had thought it was the au pair who was smoking in the house when Jake began using cannabis at the age of 15. 'We thought we were ready for a bit of pot,' said John. 'Our daughter came back from a party and was really ill from it when she was 15 and we teased her about it – of course, she never touched it again. I smoked at university, we all did, and always envisaged how I'd tackle it chummily with my kids, play the cool dad. God, how stupid. This stuff is not the same ballgame.'

Then came the school truancy and the stealing. 'All for a drug they try to tell us isn't addictive,' said Susanne. 'His life is disintegrating before our eyes.'

Debra Bell will use her real name. From South London, her son William is now 21 and also through the worst of what she believes was a skunk addiction that turned a sporty public schoolboy into a violent, aggressive thief.

'We knew about cannabis, but nothing about skunk. It was all such a shock,' she said.

'We were undermined as parents, by the Government downgrading it, by doctors not taking it seriously. William could just shrug his shoulders and say everybody at school was doing it, and it was pretty obvious in the months that followed that they were.

'My husband is a barrister and he started to see that this was a drug addiction. He began to wash his hands of him, but this was my beautiful boy... we fell out a lot over it. Guy's stance was tough and eventually we did throw him out of the house and I didn't see him for a year. It was a nightmare.'

All her efforts to get help foundered. 'The professionals were just out of date in their understanding. We felt deeply ashamed that we couldn't get

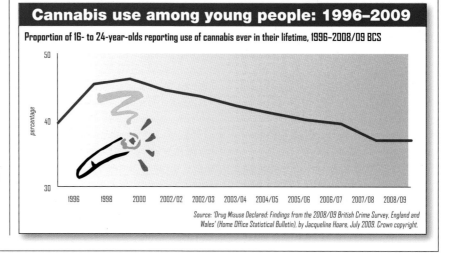

Cannabis use among young people: 1996–2009

Proportion of 16- to 24-year-olds reporting use of cannabis ever in their lifetime, 1996–2008/09 BCS

Source: 'Drug Misuse Declared: Findings from the 2008/09 British Crime Survey, England and Wales' (Home Office Statistical Bulletin), by Jacqueline Hoare, July 2009. Crown copyright.

a good outcome for our son, as he was sliding more and more into this nightmare.'

Now reconciled with William, Bell set up her own website in the end and found a flood of other families desperate for such a helpline. 'Suddenly we were just hearing all these carbon-copy stories, thousands. It is such a hidden subject, but such a huge phenomenon. No respect for class or creed or colour. I think we have betrayed our children through our ignorance. Our generation smoked, but here and there. Everybody did it – but children didn't smoke it, children whose brains were still developing.'

Whether or not there is a new middle-class phenomenon of teenagers – mostly boys but also some girls – who are at best losing great swathes of their youth and at worst endangering their mental health to the mind-numbing effects of skunk is at the moment only anecdotal. But certainly there is a huge rise in the numbers of articulate parents who are prepared to speak out about their experiences.

Strong cannabis is nothing new: its hallucinogenic effects were recorded at the beginning of civilisation and echoed in literature in stories of writers from Alexandre Dumas to Paul Bowles. But many believe that the new, hydroponically grown strain is a thoroughly modern threat to a generation who see traditionally 'addictive' drugs like heroin and crack as 'dirty', and cannabis as somehow the healthy herb despite its genetically modified new form.

In the foreword to a 1972 report to US President Richard Nixon and Congress of the National Commission on Marihuana and Drug Abuse, the commission's chairman wrote: 'Seldom in the nation's history has there been a phenomenon more divisive, more misunderstood, more fraught with impact on family, personal, and community relationships than the marihuana phenomenon.'

As the commission noted more than 30 years ago, the concept of cannabis dependency or addiction and its impact on health and psychology was highly prone to misunderstanding and disagreement, something that seems to be the same today.

Over decades, successive government committees, books, research papers, medical studies and experts have taken robust views, opposing views and speculative ones. In the US at the moment there is a movement to use cannabis to treat hyperactive primary age children, while other experts claim it has links to schizophrenia, depression and even testicular cancer.

'What is clear is that nothing is clear,' said Harry Shapiro, the director of communications at the charity Drugscope.

'There are problems associated with cannabis and nobody has ever denied that. A lot of our members who are active in young people's drug treatment services or psychiatry will of course only be seeing the worst-case scenarios. If a million or so people are using cannabis in the country, then obviously that is not the normal experience. An issue that is coming up now is this idea that cannabis is 20 or 50 times stronger than it used to be, but the forensic data makes it clear that, as more and more cannabis is grown in this country, that will be producing a stronger kind of cannabis, about twice the strength, maybe, of what you would expect from the resin of the 1970s. But you can't say that that means it is twice the danger,' he said.

Shapiro stresses that vulnerable groups or those, especially young men, with a pre-existing tendency to mental health problems, are more likely to get into difficulty with cannabis.

'But for a lot of young boys it is about wasting time. And wasting time is the biggest threat they'll face. Smoke it regularly for a couple of years and you're doing nothing else. So while obviously the mental health issues we know about are at the more dramatic end of things, there are other issues and we have to be careful and look out for the people likely to get into the most serious problems, who are those self-medicating against problems in the family, at school, with their friends.' He feels there are myths around skunk and that strong cannabis is nothing new. 'Even in the 1960s we had Nepalese temple balls and Thai sticks, the connoisseurs' cannabis if you like.'

General statistics on drug use show the heroin-using population is ageing: it is not attracting new users. But cheap alcohol and cannabis are more attractive as patterns of drug use shift. 'At the moment, skunk is supplied by gangs growing it in houses and flats, and the police are getting good at shutting those down. There is evidence there is a growing demand for imported cannabis again, so if that goes on you might just see another shift away from it.'

Many people believe that waiting for change is not enough and legislation is needed to deal with the problem. Helen Sello is in her mid-50s and her son is schizophrenic. 'I'm not sure which one thing caused the other,' she said. 'Did the schizophrenia come from the drug or was he self-medicating? It's not really a useful thing to do if you have any high risk toward mental illness, and who knows who can pick and choose?

Cannabis has been used for more than 4,000 years

'I thought it was perfectly harmless. I thought I'd prefer him to do that more than getting drunk. I support legalisation, not because I think young people take a great deal of notice of the law – they don't – but because I think that with legalisation comes control. Give people more information: vulnerable young people need to know what this drug can do. If anything makes me really angry it is that this is such a polarised debate, an immature debate. It's either that cannabis is good or it's bad.'

For Tory MP Charles Walker, the chair of the all-party parliamentary committee looking at children and cannabis, the damage that has been done both by the historical and generational tolerance of cannabis and by the Government's out-of-date attitudes has meant that a seriously dangerous drug is not recognised as such.

'I have met and spoken to so many families who have been devastated –

I mean devastated – by this drug,' he said. 'It is clearly highly addictive both psychically and psychologically and the damage is terrible: high-achieving children turning into shadows of their former selves and creating widespread misery.

'I think there is a historical legacy, which is why cannabis has been so downgraded by people in their 40s and 50s like me who don't understand that we are facing a different drug from the one everyone smoked in their youth. I wish we could change its name from cannabis to emphasise that.

'It's a hallucinogenic drug and it's having a far greater effect on the teenage mind, whose chemical make-up is so delicate. I think we need a new awareness. Better education in schools, far less tolerance from society. Let's intervene earlier and let's forget the historical legacy of our own experiences because they are obsolete. Thank God, as a parent myself, that I found out about this in order to talk to my own children before they reach their teenage years.'

But not everyone is convinced we are sitting on an enormous generational time bomb. Author Anthony Horowitz attacked what he called the 'Myerson angst' of fearful parenting. The author of the boy spy Alex Ryder books has two teenage sons. 'Frankly, we need to lighten up a bit. We need a little less angst and fear about teenage boys – after all, we have to remember they grow up to be us.'

He said he could not be a children's writer if he didn't have a belief in the essentially positive nature of young people. 'The constant demonising of them by press and Government and now by parents is a drip-drip of venom that will only erode their faith in themselves.'

A 60-year-old mother from Plymouth agrees with not giving up on the child. Her son is now 24 and lives in Wales. He began smoking cannabis on a family camping holiday at the age of 15. 'He doesn't like to come back to Plymouth now, because many of his old friends are still in their bedrooms, smoking dope. It's a nonsense that this is not an addictive drug, a nonsense. I think he felt very guilty and knew he was throwing these precious years down the drain.

'I pinned up articles in his bedroom, talked to him and talked to him. It was a four-year nightmare: he stole his sisters' pocket money, he frightened his sisters and he would kick their doors in to get money or in rage. I had thought at first "OK, he's a 15-year-old boy, he's going to dabble" – I was so innocent at first.'

But she believes she was right to wait it out until her son got fed up of wasting his life. 'Don't throw them out,' she said. 'Just love them, give them nice food, make sure they know you are there for them. Never give up on them and they'll come back to you.'

Cannabis: a history

⇨ Cannabis has been used for more than 4,000 years, including for medicinal purposes in Indian, Chinese and Middle-Eastern civilisations. In China, it has been used to treat such conditions as malaria, constipation and rheumatism.

⇨ Doctors in the West began to take an interest in its medicinal use in the middle of the 19th century. Queen Victoria was prescribed cannabis by her doctor to relieve period pain.

⇨ The drug was outlawed in the UK in 1928, following an international drugs conference in Geneva, at which an Egyptian delegate claimed that it was a threat to society and as dangerous as opium.

⇨ Recreational use in the UK began in the 1950s as migrants from the Caribbean arrived. It soared in popularity during the 'flower power' years in the 1960s.

⇨ A Home Office investigation in 1968 concluded: 'There is no evidence that this activity is causing violent crime or aggression, anti-social behaviour, or is producing in otherwise normal people conditions of dependence or psychosis requiring medical treatment.'

⇨ Advanced cultivation techniques have led to an increase in potency over the past 20 years. Average levels of THC (tetrahydrocannabinol, the main psychoactive ingredient) in marijuana sold in America rose from 3.5% in 1988 to 8.5% in 2006. 'Skunk' is the most potent strain and now dominates the UK market, according to Home Office research.

⇨ This article first appeared in the *Observer*, 15 March 2009.

Helpline tells children 'pot safer than alcohol'

Children calling the Government's drugs helpline are being told that cannabis is safer than alcohol and that ecstasy will not damage their health, an investigation by the *Sunday Telegraph* has found

Advisers manning the FRANK helpline are informing callers they believed to be children as young as 13 that alcohol is a 'much more powerful drug than cannabis' and that using the illegal drug recreationally is not harmful because it 'doesn't get you that high'.

Callers are also being told that taking ecstasy will not lead to long-term damage and that if they are in doubt, to 'just take half a pill and if you are handling that OK, you can take the other half'.

They are even being told that they would be able to smoke a cannabis joint, on top of ecstasy, with no ill-effects.

The advice, given to reporters who rang the helpline posing as young people, has alarmed anti-drugs campaigners who branded it 'scandalous' and 'irresponsible'.

Health experts have condemned the advice given to children as 'frankly appalling', 'factually incorrect' and 'worryingly cavalier'.

After being presented with the findings, the Government last night said it had launched an immediate investigation into the FRANK service, which is funded by three separate departments, and said it would

By Julie Henry, David Barrett and Alex Ralph

be taking action against advisers involved.

Chris Grayling, the shadow Home Secretary, said: 'The idea that the Government's helpline should be saying to young people "go for it" and that cannabis should be class C when it has just been classified by the Government as class B, shows that the Home Office is all over the place in its approach to drugs.'

Professor Neil McKeganey, professor of drug misuse research at Glasgow University, said: 'Having read one of the transcripts, it is extraordinary that the FRANK councillor seems more concerned to place cannabis smoking in some kind of comfort zone of acceptable behaviour rather than address the risks of such drug use on the part of a 13-year-old child.'

Mary Brett, a spokesman for the Talking About Cannabis charity, said: 'It is scandalous. These people are talking to kids, for goodness sake. Taking drugs can trigger all kinds of psychosis in people that have a genetic predisposition to it. Why are they not told that? Medical experts have said

time and again that skunk, the newer type of cannabis that many young people are taking, is dangerous.

'These children are being told they can choose. But the risky bit of their brains develops before the inhibitory bit of their brain and they take risks.

'They have to be told "this is not for you". When they hear fair, reasoned arguments against, they respond. It is obvious they are not hearing them from FRANK.'

An estimated five million people in the UK are users of illegal or street drugs

The helpline, established by the Government in 2003 with £3 million funding, was described in a Home Office drugs strategy recently as 'the key channel by which Government communicates the dangers of drugs, including cannabis, to young people'.

But in calls to its helpline, manned 24 hours a day, seven days a week, reporters posing as teenagers were told by different advisers that drug taking was not harmful.

At no point in the conversations did the FRANK team try to dissuade the callers from taking drugs.

The effects on the body were played down to the extent that one adviser, referring to ecstasy, said: 'At the end of the day I know where you're coming from – doing a pill and it felt great.'

Another councillor said that cannabis, a class B drug, should be regarded as class C and that 'cannabis doesn't really get you that high. You know you are always in control'.

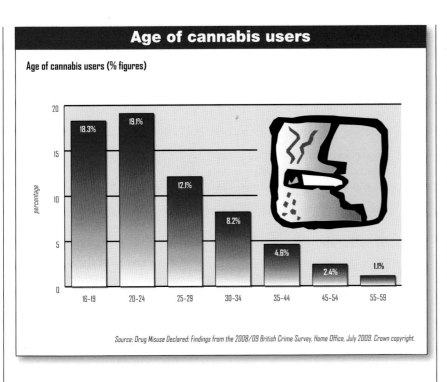

Age of cannabis users

Age of cannabis users (% figures)

- 16-19: 18.3%
- 20-24: 19.1%
- 25-29: 12.1%
- 30-34: 8.2%
- 35-44: 4.6%
- 45-54: 2.4%
- 55-59: 1.1%

Source: Drug Misuse Declared: Findings from the 2008/09 British Crime Survey, Home Office, July 2009. Crown copyright.

A third adviser stated: 'Nicotine is physically addictive. Cannabis isn't. You can stop smoking it any time you want.'

Alcohol was presented as a much greater danger than illegal drugs, including heroin, more expensive and with many more negative effects.

One adviser told a caller: 'The withdrawals of alcohol are worse than heroin for example; people can die when they become addicted to alcohol and stop suddenly.'

The reporters were also told that the police 'would not do anything' if they found a young person with cannabis and that if they are caught with pills, they should say they were for their own use to avoid being prosecuted as a dealer.

In one call, where the reporter claimed to be the friend of a 13-year-old boy who had started smoking cannabis, the adviser said: 'He won't get addicted, no. Tell him you spoke to FRANK and they told me it's not as dangerous as alcohol. Tell him they said by using it recreationally, it's not as bad as alcohol, because that's the truth in terms of the power of the drug.'

He went on to say that if alcohol was illegal, it would be a class A drug, the most harmful category, whereas 'cannabis should just be a class C drug'.

Another reporter, posing as a 15-year-old girl who had taken her first ecstasy tablet, asked if it would affect her health in any way.

The response was 'Nah'. He told the caller that he could not say 'go and take Es, you're absolutely fine', but that 'in terms of taking a pill like that, it's not going to affect your health'.

He went on to say 'obviously you had a really good experience. It's like most things, if you do it in moderation, you lessen your chances.

'A good idea is if you don't know what it is you are taking, take a half a one and see how you go and if you are handling that OK, you can take the other half.'

The adviser was also unsure what classification the class A drug was.

During a discussion where the adviser talked about mixing drugs, the reporter asked if it was safe to have cannabis after taking an ecstasy pill.

The adviser said: 'Again, I'm not condoning it but it wouldn't spin you out like another pill or powder. If you're asking me if you could have a spliff with it, would it have any major effects, generally speaking, no, although people are individuals so what works for one might not work for another, but generally speaking, no, you'd be able to have a spliff with it.'

An estimated five million people in the UK are users of illegal or street drugs.

Health experts are growing in-creasingly worried about the effects on young people's mental health. There is also growing evidence that contrary to earlier assumptions, cannabis can be addictive.

Varieties of skunk, which contain much higher levels of tetra-hydrocannabinol (THC), the active chemical, are more dangerous than the cannabis used in the 1960s and 1970s but are now widespread and often the choice of young people.

Dr Zerrin Atakan, consultant psychiatrist at the Institute of Psychiatry, said: 'Any drug use while the brain is still developing may lead to structural or functional changes. One Australian study has shown that heavy cannabis users show clear structural abnormalities of the brain.

'Another recent study has also shown that cannabis use before 18 can lead to abnormalities in areas of the brain that control memory, attention, decision-making and language skills.

'Also, contrary to previously held beliefs, it is now considered that regular users can develop "tolerance" to the drug, one of the main characteristics of addiction. Regular users require higher doses to become "stoned". Some people find it very hard to give it up and become highly anxious if they do.'

According to the Home Office, drug use among all ages, including young people, has fallen in recent years. The Government, which downgraded cannabis to a grade C drug in 2004, has recently reclassified it to B.

A Government spokesman said: 'It is completely unacceptable for a FRANK adviser to be giving out wrong, misleading and inaccurate information. We are urgently looking into the matter and will identify the person or persons involved and take action.

'FRANK is an important resource for young people who need help and advice about drugs. It is vital that FRANK advisers give out correct and straightforward advice – we have therefore commissioned a review of the training advisers receive and will act upon it.'

18 April 2009

Cannabis and the risks

Facts you need to know

By Dr Mark Porter,
Times Correspondent

I used to have fairly liberal views on cannabis and have compared it favourably in the past with alcohol and tobacco, both of which exact a bigger toll on our society than all illegal drugs combined. But, along with most doctors, I have become increasingly concerned in recent years that the drug is much more dangerous than we thought, and certainly nowhere near as safe as most teenagers still think.

The days are gone when sensible people argue that cannabis is harmless

The days are gone when sensible people argue that cannabis is harmless. The evidence that has been collected over the past decade shows that it is clearly not, although for most of the three to four million people in the UK who dabble the risks are still small. The vast majority are occasional users who, with time, will eventually turn their backs on the drug and emerge unscathed. This is in stark contrast to the outlook for the tens of millions who use cigarettes and alcohol – two legal drugs that kill, maim and injure more people in a weekend than cannabis does in a year. But there are two groups who seem particularly vulnerable to the harmful effects of cannabis: heavy users and those who used the drug at an early age.

Like all parents I like to think that my teenage daughters are sensible enough to avoid drugs, but I am realistic enough to know that if they haven't tried cannabis already then there is a good chance that they will. Statistics show that young children are almost as likely to experiment with cannabis as with tobacco. According to a recent survey by the Schools Health Education Unit, one 12-year-old in 16 and one 15-year-old in four now admits to having tried cannabis

at least once, up from one in 100 and one in 50 respectively in 1987.

The Government has responded to growing concerns among doctors by performing a U-turn on previous policy and last month upgraded cannabis from class C to class B under the Misuse of Drugs Act, a message that it hopes will not go unheeded by young people.

I have never been convinced that the legal status of cannabis makes any real difference to whether a teenager tries it. It has more to do with peer attitudes, and the overriding belief among teenagers today is that cannabis is a bit of harmless fun – the most dangerous thing about a joint being the tobacco that the grass or resin is mixed with. They are mistaken.

Here are a few key facts that all teenagers (and their parents) should be made aware of:
Cannabis damages the lungs: Most people consider cannabis to be much safer than tobacco but, drag for drag,

it is actually more harmful. Cannabis smoke is far more acrid than tobacco and causes more damage to the lining of the airways. The British Lung Foundation estimates that smoking an admittedly hefty three to four joints a day causes the same level of damage as smoking 20 cigarettes a day. And, like tobacco, it is packed with carcinogens.

Chest physicians are reporting that a growing number of cannabis users appear to be developing the sort of lung damage normally seen only in middle-aged and elderly smokers – and up to 20 years earlier. And it doesn't seem to make much difference how you smoke it. Research into the relative 'safety' of the various smoking devices – joints, bongs, vaporisers and water pipes – found no significant difference in the harmful chemicals inhaled. Because water pipes filter out some of the ingredient (THC) that makes users high, they tend to inhale more of the harmful components to get a decent hit.

Cannabis can cause irreversible changes in the brain: The most alarming discovery in recent years has been that cannabis can trigger serious mental illness such as schizophrenia.

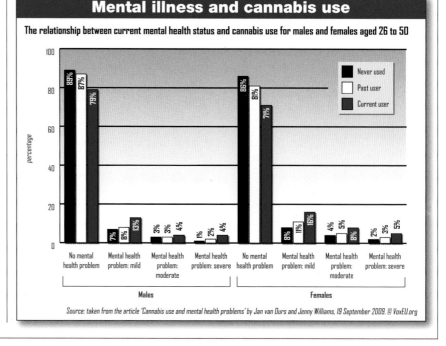

Mental illness and cannabis use

The relationship between current mental health status and cannabis use for males and females aged 26 to 50

Source: taken from the article 'Cannabis use and mental health problems' by Jan van Ours and Jenny Williams, 19 September 2009. © VoxEU.org

As a rough rule of thumb the average person's lifetime risk of developing schizophrenia is about one in 100. This risk increases to about one in 30 in occasional cannabis users and closer to one in 15 in regular users (at least once a day).

The brains of teenagers appear to be particularly susceptible to the drug: A recent study in New Zealand found that children who started to use cannabis before the age of 15 were nearly five times more likely to develop serious mental illness by their late twenties, compared with those who started at 18. Neuroscientists suspect that the greater susceptibility of young teenagers is because the brain continues to develop during the teen years. Drug use is thought to influence this final phase of brain formation, increasing the risk of the type of functional and chemical imbalances associated with conditions such as schizophrenia.

The problem is compounded because most of the cannabis sold in Britain today is much more potent than that of a decade ago. These stronger variants (skunk) contain far more of THC, the active ingredient, which is thought to induce psychosis, and far less of another ingredient (cannabidiol) found in standard varieties, which is anti-psychotic and protects the brain. But neurochemical changes don't alter behaviour alone. Tests on mice suggest that they can also permanently disrupt a developing brain's ability to remember things, even after the drug is withdrawn. It is difficult to draw comparisons with human development, but scientists in the field believe that exposure before the age of 15 could cause lasting memory deficit.

Cannabis can be addictive: Contrary to street lore that you cannot become addicted to cannabis, one user in ten develops some form of dependence, with abstinence leading to craving and withdrawal effects. Cannabis abuse now accounts for ten per cent of attendances at UK drug treatment centres.

Most of the cannabis sold in Britain today is much more potent than that of a decade ago

Is it a gateway to more dangerous drugs? This is a controversial area. There is little doubt that cannabis users are more likely to try harder drugs such as cocaine and heroin, but this gateway effect is much smaller than we used to think. While most hard drug users start off trying cannabis, most cannabis users don't end up on hard drugs. Only one cannabis user in 25 admits to having tried heroin. That said, the social factors of mixing with peers who are using drugs and having access to supply can only make progression more likely. Age is again a factor – younger cannabis smokers are more likely to move on to hard drugs.

Cannabis and your bones: Recent work indicates that cannabis may accelerate the thinning of the skeleton that occurs as we age. Bone is a living tissue that is constantly being remodelled; cells called osteoblasts lay down bone while osteoclasts dissolve it. Careful balancing of the activities of both groups of cells mean that overall bone mass remains steady – at least until the age of 40 – despite our entire skeleton being replaced every seven years.

Researchers from Aberdeen University have discovered that chemicals found in cannabis may upset this delicate balance in favour of the osteoclasts and bone resorption, leading to osteoporosis – a condition now thought to affect one woman in three, and one man in ten, over the age of 50.

Cannabis and sex: Little is known about the impact of cannabis on sexual function but there is growing anecdotal evidence that it may be linked to shrinking of the testicles and low sex drive in men. Research published this week suggests that it may increase the odds of developing testicular cancer. More research is needed but should any of these links be proved they could become the most powerful deterrent of all for boys and men.

Nothing in life is totally risk-free and all these potential hazards need to be put in context – the vast majority of people who try cannabis will come through the experience unscathed. But for some, particularly those who use it regularly, it will leave a permanent scar that could cost them their friends, family, career and possibly even their lives. At the moment we have no reliable way of identifying those most at risk but we do know that the earlier you start the more dangerous the drug is likely to be.

This article first appeared in the Times, *14 February 2009*

© Dr Mark Porter

Cannabis: the law has changed

Information from the Home Office

The law has changed.

Cannabis has been reclassified up from a class C to a class B drug.

This means that there are more severe penalties for people caught in the possession of cannabis.

If you are 18 and over and caught with cannabis

If you are caught with cannabis, the police will take action.

You can be arrested – even if it is the first time that you have been caught.

Maturing female cannabis plant

As well as confiscating your cannabis, the agreed police response will be to:
- ⇨ Give you a cannabis warning if it is the first time you have been caught with cannabis.
- ⇨ Give you a Penalty Notice for Disorder if it is the second time you have been caught with cannabis. This is an on-the-spot fine of £80.
- ⇨ Arrest you if it is the third or more time you have been caught with

cannabis. If you are convicted of possession, you can be sentenced to a maximum of five years in prison and given an unlimited fine. You will also have a criminal record.

If you are between ten and 17

If you are caught with cannabis, the police will take action. You can be arrested – even if it is the first time that you have been caught. You can also be referred to a Youth Offending Team at any stage.

As well as confiscating your cannabis, the agreed police response will be to:
- ⇨ Give you a reprimand if it is the first time you have been caught with cannabis.
- ⇨ Give you a final warning and refer you to a Youth Offending Team if it is the second time you have been caught with cannabis.
- ⇨ Arrest you if it is the third or more time you have been caught with cannabis. If you are convicted of possession, you can be sentenced to a maximum of five years in prison and given an unlimited fine. You will also have a criminal record.

If there are aggravating factors present the police will escalate their response accordingly.

If you supply cannabis to other people

If the police think that you are dealing cannabis, they will arrest you. If you are convicted of supplying or intending to supply cannabis, you can be sentenced to a maximum of 14 years in prison and given an unlimited fine. If you sell cannabis near schools, you can get a stiffer prison sentence.

The risks of using cannabis

Using cannabis can harm both your physical and mental health. There is already evidence that cannabis use is associated with a higher risk of future mental health problems. These health risks could be worse if you are young, you smoke a lot and you smoke strong cannabis, like skunk.

What are the risks?

Cannabis:
- ⇨ can make you become anxious, panicky, suspicious and paranoid;
- ⇨ affects your co-ordination;
- ⇨ increases your heart rate and affects your blood pressure;
- ⇨ can cause lung disease and may increase the risk of cancer in long-term heavy users;
- ⇨ can affect your fertility;
- ⇨ can make you feel lethargic and sap your motivation.

What are the risks to your mental health?

There is evidence that regular cannabis users have an increased risk of developing serious mental health problems, including schizophrenia. It is possible that using strong cannabis, like skunk, might increase these risks. You don't know how it will affect your mental health in the future.

You shouldn't take cannabis at all if you've a history of mental health problems, depression or paranoia.

⇨ The above information is reprinted with kind permission from the Home Office. Visit http://drugs.homeoffice.gov.uk for more information.

© Crown copyright

Cannabis and psychosis

Re-classification of cannabis will have minimal impact on incidence of psychosis says study

Thousands of people would need to stop using cannabis in order to prevent a single case of schizophrenia, according to a new study from the University of Bristol.

The research follows last year's decision by the UK Government to reclassify the drug from class C to class B, partly out of concerns that cannabis, especially the more potent varieties, may increase the risk of schizophrenia in young people. However, the evidence for the relationship between cannabis and schizophrenia or psychosis remains controversial.

The Bristol scientists, with colleagues from the University of Cambridge and the London School of Hygiene and Tropical Medicine, took the latest information on numbers of cannabis users, the risk of developing schizophrenia, and the risk that cannabis use causes schizophrenia to estimate how many cannabis users may need to be stopped to prevent one case of schizophrenia.

The study found it would be necessary to stop 2,800 heavy cannabis users in young men and over 5,000 heavy cannabis users in young women to prevent a single case of schizophrenia. Among light cannabis users, those numbers rise to over 10,000 young men and nearly 30,000 young women to prevent one case of schizophrenia.

That's just part of the story. Interventions to prevent cannabis use typically do not succeed for every person who is treated. Depending on how effective an intervention is at preventing cannabis use, it would be necessary to treat even higher numbers of users to achieve the thousands of successful results necessary to prevent a very few cases of schizophrenia.

Dr Matthew Hickman, one of the authors of the report published last week in the journal *Addiction*, said:

'Preventing cannabis use is important for many reasons, including reducing tobacco and drug dependence and improving school performance. But our evidence suggests that focusing on schizophrenia may have been misguided. Our research cannot resolve the question whether cannabis causes schizophrenia, but does show that many people need to give up cannabis in order to have an impact on the number of people with schizophrenia. The likely impact of reclassifying cannabis in the UK on schizophrenia or psychosis incidence is very uncertain.'

Paper:
Hickman M., Vickerman P., Macleod J., Lewis G., Zammit S., Kirkbride J., Jones P. 'If cannabis caused schizophrenia – how many cannabis users may need to be prevented in order to prevent one case of schizophrenia? England and Wales calculations'. *Addiction* 2009; 104: 1856–1861
4 November 2009

⇨ Information from the University of Bristol. Visit www.bristol.ac.uk for more information.
© University of Bristol

Poll reveals anger at cannabis law

The reclassification of cannabis appears to have provoked widespread irritation

There is a substantial amount of anger over the Government's decision to reclassify cannabis, a politics.co.uk poll suggests.

The poll, which comes as government ministers from across the world meet in Vienna for the UN's summit on drugs, shows a deep split in public opinion over how to proceed with narcotics legislation.

Asked if drugs should be legalised, just under 50 per cent of respondents answered 'yes', while 37 per cent said 'no'.

But opinions on the reclassification of cannabis were far clearer.

13 per cent of users agreed with the decision, compared to 87 per cent who said they 'disagreed' or 'strongly disagreed'.

The Government recently implemented the change to cannabis, bringing it back up to class B after former Home Secretary David Blunkett expended considerable political capital downgrading it to class C in 2003.

But the poll showed considerably less sympathy towards calls from the Government's own Advisory Council on the Misuse of Drugs to downgrade ecstasy.

Over 50 per cent of users said they disagreed with the decision, while 37 per cent agreed.

Asked what they thought of current UK drugs policy, politics.co.uk users appeared to take a liberal stance. 62 per cent of users said current policy was too authoritarian. That compared to 25 per cent, who said it was too lenient.
11 March 2009

⇨ The above information is reprinted with kind permission from politics.co.uk. Visit www.politics.co.uk for more information.
© Adfero

David Nutt: my views on drugs classification

David Nutt, the Government's former chief drugs adviser, on how he formulated his controversial views on drugs

Formulating policy in relation to drugs is obviously quite a difficult thing to do. I comment on it, as I always have, from the perspective of a psychiatrist who is interested in drugs and drugs and their effect on the brain.

We have a range of expertise on the Advisory Council on the Misuse of Drugs (ACMD); we're very strong in terms of chemistry and pharmacology, and psychology; and we have a definite knowledge, interest and responsibility to look at social harms as well. We provide one arm of the policy-formulating perspective. In addition, there are a number of other agencies, organisations and individuals who contribute to policy formation.

There are also international partners – we have signed up to international treaties – which determine that, in essence, the UK follows United Nations policy on drugs. This can be quite a tough constraining influence on how countries regulate drugs (although some countries, such as the Netherlands, have managed to be more flexible, even though they still sign up to the international conventions).

Then, of course, there are other factors feeding into political decisions about drugs: what the general public thinks (or is thought to think); and then there's the media. In recent years, the whole process of determining drug classification has become quite complex and highly politicised.

Cannabis – a potent problem

I am going to focus on cannabis because it is the only drug that has been downgraded in the history of the 1971 Misuse of Drugs Act, an interesting point in itself. The issues relating to cannabis pose a challenge to whether the act is working as it was originally intended.

The ACMD was requested by the Home Secretary in 2007 to review the status of cannabis because: 'Though statistics show that cannabis use has fallen significantly, there is real public concern about the potential mental health effects of cannabis use, in particular the use of stronger forms of the drug, commonly known as skunk.'

So there was a skunk scare. Cannabis had gone from class B to C, but, supposedly, skunk use had been increasing and it was getting stronger, so we were asked to review whether the decision to go from B to C was still appropriate. In our report we came to several conclusions:

⇨ Cannabis is a harmful drug and there are concerns about the widespread use of cannabis amongst young people.
⇨ A concerted public health response is required to drastically reduce its use.
⇨ Current evidence suggests a probable, but weak, causal link between psychotic illness and cannabis use.
⇨ The harms caused by cannabis are not considered to be as serious as drugs in class B and therefore it should remain a class C drug.

There has been a lot of commentary and some research as to whether cannabis is associated with schizophrenia, and the results are really quite difficult to interpret. What we can say is that cannabis use is associated with an increased experience of psychotic disorders. That is quite a complicated thing to disentangle because, of course, the reason people take cannabis is that it produces a change in their mental state. These changes are akin to being psychotic – they include distortions of perception, especially in visual and auditory perception, as well as in the

way one thinks. So it can be quite hard to know whether, when you analyse the incidence of psychotic disorders with cannabis, you are simply looking at the acute effects of cannabis, as opposed to some consequence of cannabis use.

If we look on the generous side there is a likelihood that taking cannabis, particularly if you use a lot of it, will make you more prone to having psychotic experiences. That includes schizophrenia, but schizophrenia is a relatively rare condition so it's very hard to be sure about its causation. The analysis we came up with was that smokers of cannabis are about 2.6 times more likely to have a psychotic-like experience than non-smokers. To put that figure in proportion, you are 20 times more likely to get lung cancer if you smoke tobacco than if you don't.

There is a relatively small risk for smoking cannabis and psychotic illness compared with quite a substantial risk for smoking tobacco and lung cancer.

The other paradox is that schizophrenia seems to be disappearing (from the general population) even though cannabis use has increased markedly in the last 30 years. When we were reviewing the general practice research database in the UK from the University of Keele, research consistently and clearly showed that psychosis and schizophrenia are still on the decline. So, even though skunk has been around now for ten years, there has been no upswing in schizophrenia. In fact, where people have looked, they haven't found any evidence linking cannabis use in a population and schizophrenia.

Media bias

I want to move on now to look at how people gather information

about drugs and the challenges of communicating the best evidence relating to drug harms to the public. This is difficult in the face of what you might call a peculiar media imbalance in relation to drugs. The following data illustrates a remarkable finding. It derives from the PhD of a Scottish graduate, Alasdair JM Forsyth, who looked at every single newspaper report of drug deaths in Scotland from 1990 to 1999 and compared them with the coroners' data.

Over the decade, there were 2,255 drug deaths, of which the Scottish newspapers reported 546. For aspirin, only one in every 265 deaths were reported. For morphine, one in 72 deaths were reported, indicating that editors were not interested in this opiate. They were more interested in heroin, where one in five deaths were reported, and methadone, where one in 16 deaths were reported.

They were also more interested in stimulants. With amphetamines, deaths are relatively rare at 36, but one in three were reported; for cocaine it was one in eight. Amazingly, almost every single ecstasy death – that is, 26 out of 28 of those where ecstasy was named as a possible contributory factor – was reported. So there's a peculiar imbalance in terms of reporting that is clearly inappropriate in relation to the relative harms of ecstasy compared with other drugs. The reporting gives the impression that ecstasy is a much more dangerous drug than it is. This is one of the reasons I wrote the article about horse riding that caused such extreme media

reactions earlier this year. The other thing you'll notice is that there is a drug missing, and that's cannabis. Also missing is alcohol, which will have killed a similar number – 2,000 to 3,000 people – in Scotland over that time, maybe more. Of course, cannabis wouldn't have killed anyone because it doesn't kill. And that's one of the reasons why we thought cannabis should be class C, because you cannot die of cannabis overdose.

Assessing harm

We've tried very hard for at least the last ten years to put together a structure for assessing drug harms. This eventually became a research paper, *Development of a Rational Scale to Assess the Harms of Drugs of Potential Misuse*, published in the *Lancet* in 2007. Despite – or perhaps because of – its novelty and remit, it was very hard to get a paper published that challenged some of the current (mis) perceptions about drugs.

In principle, we broke down drug harms into the following parameters: physical harm (acute, chronic and intravenous), dependency (intensity of pleasure, psychological dependence, physical dependence), and social harms (intoxication, other social harms and healthcare costs).

We looked at all the drugs in the Misuse of Drugs Act and added some others that weren't already covered by it. For example, we included ketamine, which wasn't covered by the act at the time, solvents, and tobacco and alcohol, because we thought it was very important that harms of illicit

drugs were assessed against the harms of drugs that people know and use. This analysis eventually established a ranking order.

A number of important points emerged. The ranking suggested that there are clearly some very harmful drugs (you might say these would be class A drugs) and there are some drugs that aren't very harmful, such as khat or alkyl nitrites, which aren't controlled by the act at all.

Interestingly, some class A drugs scored much lower than other class A drugs, suggesting that there is some anomaly in terms of that part of the current statutory classification system.

The ranking also suggests that a tripartite classification system might make sense, with drugs ranking as more harmful than alcohol being class A and those ranking lower than tobacco as class C. The exercise also highlighted how dangerous alcohol is. I believe that dealing with the harms of alcohol is probably the biggest challenge that we have in relation to drug harms today.

One problem is that sometimes you get into what I think of as an illegality-logic loop. This is an example of a conversation I've had many times with many people, some of them politicians:

MP: 'You can't compare harms from a legal activity with an illegal one.'
Professor Nutt: 'Why not?'
MP: 'Because one's illegal.'
Professor Nutt: 'Why is it illegal?'
MP: 'Because it's harmful.'
Professor Nutt: 'Don't we need to compare harms to determine if it should be illegal?'
MP: 'You can't compare harms from a legal activity with an illegal one.'

I have been surprised how difficult this concept is to get across to some people, whether they are politicians, fellow scientists or members of the general public.

⇨ This is an edited extract from a July 2009 lecture by Professor David Nutt, a transcript of which was published last week by the Centre for Crime and Justice Studies at Kings College London. crimeandjustice. org.uk/estimatingdrugharms.html
3 November 2009
© *Guardian Newspapers Limited 2009*

Politicians intoxicated by cowardice in drugs debate

Nutt was the victim of an outdated taboo that neither Johnson nor Cameron appear to have the courage to challenge

By Simon Jenkins

Even Alan Johnson must know his sacking of David Nutt was a mistake. The boast that he was being 'big enough, strong enough, bold enough' to make such decisions was a gift to the gods of hypocrisy. If he was that big and strong he would have ignored Nutt and not pretended that an academic lecture on drug classification constituted a 'public campaign' against him. Nutt's Advisory Council on the Misuse of Drugs had been humiliated by Johnson and his colleagues, and rendered virtually useless. Leave the guy alone.

It is not the mistakes politicians make that matter, but why they make them. The Labour Government's drugs policy must qualify as the worst confection of unreason even in Whitehall's copious canon. This is not for want of advice or research. Few subjects have been more rigorously investigated, not least by Nutt and his collapsed committee.

We know the differential impact of narcotics on the brain. We chart the evolution of schizophrenia in drug users. We can measure harm reduction schemes across Europe. We can even balance the impact of education against deterrence in curbing drug use. When I hear of another committee, conference or seminar on drugs policy I scream: 'Don't waste the money: spend it on rehab instead.'

Researching drug use is pointless since policy on the subject has nothing to do with evidence, only emotion. It has to do with fear of the unknown, the taboo of other people's escapist narcotics (or worse, those of one's children). Politicians could not care less what experts say – witness this week's smattering of support for Johnson. They care only for the right-wing press, whose editors suffer a similar taboo.

The test was how the Tories reacted to Nutt's sacking. Faced with a Home Secretary gasping for air, Cameron and his home affairs spokesman, Chris Grayling, rushed forward with oxygen. Parting company with half the cabinet and the weight of scientific opinion, Cameron had a bad attack of funk. He refused to defend Nutt, and asserted his conviction that ecstasy was as harmful as heroin and crack cocaine. This was the same Cameron who, as a backbench member of the home affairs select committee in 2001,

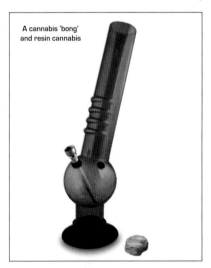

A cannabis 'bong' and resin cannabis

had supported Nutt in taking the opposite view. He must know what he said this week was rubbish.

All these politicians accept in private that the law is in chronic need of reform. Yet should they dare murmur so, they seem terrified of being assailed by the *Mail*, the *Sun* and the *Telegraph*. They could handle the House of Commons. They could even carry their constituents. But the right-wing press holds them in thrall, perhaps because they feel powerless before its lash. Might their youthful indiscretions be discovered, or the

antics of their children pursued?

Politicians can stand the pressure of corpses piling up in Helmand, but one corpse at a rave would be too much for their consciences. Whenever I have tackled Home Office ministers, from Jack Straw and Charles Clarke to recent, less distinguished holders of the office, the response is the same. Don't even think about it, they cry. We would be crucified by the press. Just say no to drugs reform.

I served on the 2000 police foundation committee on the 1971 Misuse of Drugs Act, the only exhaustive study of the act ever undertaken. It was set up with the Government's blessing and members included David Nutt, distinguished pharmacologists and two chief police officers. Our conclusions were mild, embracing a redirection of drugs policy towards harm reduction and a partial decriminalisation of cannabis use.

Polling evidence showed a wide gulf between a public desire for toughness on hard drugs on the one hand, and on the other, two-thirds of opinion that regarded cannabis as 'least harmful'. An overwhelming majority thought chasing cannabis users was 'not a police priority', and a significant majority, from all ages and social groups, favoured cannabis decriminalisation. That was confirmed in other similar polls.

What happened next was a textbook case of Tony Blair's governing style. The Home Secretary, Jack Straw, went ape, reputedly on the instructions of Alastair Campbell, then at the height of his Downing Street ascendancy. They feared that the slightest welcome for the report's findings might have the Government castigated by the right-wing press, of which Campbell lived in perpetual fear. The committee's chairman, Ruth Runciman, was summoned in advance of publication and castigated by Straw in front of his team, until Mo Mowlam had to suggest it might be better if they all read the document first.

When the report appeared it was well received. The *Daily Mail*, in a front-page editorial, welcomed it and said it had delivered 'a mature and serious national debate'. The *Telegraph* was even more favourable and criticised Straw for 'misjudging the public mood'. The head of the Metropolitan police was supportive.

In other words it was quite untrue that the public and press were opposed to drugs law reform. Realising this, Straw performed a U-turn and was induced, apparently by Campbell, to write an article full of wishy-washy assertions for the *News of the World*.

It warmly welcomed the report and further debate. There was none. The subject was buried.

The incident was a classic example of public policy determined by ministers trying to second-guess Fleet Street. Drugs policy is desperately important. It has the power to wreck lives, families and communities. It underpins a third of crime and 80% of acquisitive crime. Four decades of illegality have done nothing to curb consumption, merely breeding the most lucrative, untaxed product market in Britain. No country has achieved the remotest success with prohibition, but Britain's archaic laws have been the least successful. Go to any deprived area, any difficult school, any failing social service, and the root cause of trouble is drugs.

There is no evidence that the public is averse to reform of the 1971 law, indeed the opposite. Why senior politicians should accord mystical influence to a few irrationalist newspaper editorialists is bizarre. Ministers and opposition leaders disregard the press on war and peace, on indulging banks, and on infringing civil liberties. The media's bluff is called every day on some topic or other – and rightly so. The press, like the Pope, can field no divisions.

So what is it about drugs? Britain's deepest social problem is blighted by political cowardice towards an outdated taboo. But who will break the spell?
3 November 2009
© *Guardian Newspapers Limited 2009*

The phoney war on drugs – summary

Information from the Centre for Policy Studies

⇨ The Government has repeatedly declared that it is fighting a War on Drugs. The data presented here show that this is a Phoney War.
⇨ It is currently spending £1.5 billion a year on its drugs policy. Yet enforcement of drugs laws is weak and underfunded, while treatment policy is counter-productive.
⇨ The UK drug problem is the worst in Europe. The UK has one of the highest levels of recreational drug use. There are over ten Problem Drug Users (PDUs) per 1,000 of the adult population, compared to 4.5 in Sweden or 3.2 in the Netherlands.
⇨ The UK has one of the most liberal drug policies in Europe. Both Sweden and the Netherlands (despite popular misconceptions) have a more rigorous approach.
⇨ The UK faces a widening and a deepening crisis. Over the last ten years, class A consumption and 'problem drug use' have risen dramatically, drug use has

By Kathy Gyngell

spread to rural areas and the age of children's initiation into drugs has dropped. 41% of 15-year-olds, and 11% of 11-year-olds, have taken drugs.

The UK has one of the highest levels of recreational drug use in Europe

⇨ Drug death rates continue to rise and are far higher than the European average. The UK has 47.5 deaths per million population (aged 15 to 64) compared to 22.0 in Sweden and 9.6 in the Netherlands.

Government policy
⇨ The election of the Labour

Government in 1997 marked a new direction for drug policy. It developed a 'harm reduction' strategy which aimed to reduce the cost of problem drug use.
⇨ The focus was switched from combating all illicit drug use to the problems of PDUs. Cannabis was declassified. Drug misusing youngsters were now to be 'supported' by various agencies. Spending on methadone treatment increased threefold between 2003 and 2008.
⇨ The aim of treatment for drug offenders was no longer abstinence but management of their addiction with the aim of reducing their reoffending. In practice, this meant prescribing methadone.

⇨ Government targets were imposed on new quangos such as the National Treatment Agency in an attempt to increase the numbers of PDUs in treatment (which for most people meant methadone prescription).

⇨ Of the 200,000 addicts currently in treatment, only 6,700 have undergone in-patient treatment (i.e. short detoxification stays), and only 4,300 have had residential rehabilitation.

⇨ A Drug Intervention Programme was introduced to direct those guilty of drugs-related offences (i.e. acquisitive crime such as shop-lifting) into treatment (again, this meant in practice prescribing methadone). There is little evidence that this has been effective.

⇨ This harm-reduction approach has failed. It has entrapped 147,000 people in state-sponsored addiction. Despite the £10 billion spent on the War on Drugs, the numbers emerging from Government treatment programmes are at the same level as if there had been no treatment programme at all.

Weak enforcement and prevention

⇨ The UK drugs market is estimated to be worth £5 billion a year.

⇨ In comparison, the Government is spending only £380 million a year – or 28% of the total drugs budget – attempting to control the supply of drugs (over £800 million is spent on treatment programmes and reducing drug-related crime). Only five boats now patrol the UK's 7,750 mile coastline.

⇨ The numbers of recorded offences for importing, supply and possession of illicit drugs have all fallen over the last ten years.

⇨ At the same time, seizures of drugs have fallen and drug prices have dropped to record lows. The quantity of heroin, cocaine and cannabis that has been seized coming into the UK has fallen by 68%, 16% and 34%, respectively.

⇨ It is now accepted (even by the Government) that SOCA, the new agency established in 2006 to confront the drugs trade, has been a failure.

An alternative

⇨ Both Sweden and the Netherlands have far more coherent and effective drugs policies. These are based on:
   ↳ the enforcement of the drug laws;
   ↳ the prevention of all illicit drug use;
   ↳ the provision of addiction care.

⇨ All of these principles have been lost sight of over the last ten years in the UK.

⇨ While the UK spends the majority of its drug budget on its so-called treatment programmes, both the Netherlands and Sweden spend most of their drugs budget on prevention and enforcement. Their drugs problems are a half and a third of the size of the UK's, respectively.

⇨ Labour's War on Drugs has not, despite the rhetoric to the contrary, been fought. It has been a Phoney War – and an expensive failure.

⇨ A successful UK drug policy would:
   ↳ focus on the illicit use of all drugs, not the harms caused by drug use;
   ↳ abandon the harm reduction approach;
   ↳ develop treatment support aimed at abstinence and rehabilitation;
   ↳ include a far tougher, better-funded enforcement programme to reduce the supply of drugs.

May 2009

⇨ The above information is reprinted with kind permission from the Centre for Policy Studies. Visit www.cps.org.uk for more information.

The streets don't care what class drugs are

Upgrading cannabis and downgrading ecstasy will make no difference to policing their misuse

Cannabis was reclassified yesterday from C to B. The Advisory Council on the Misuse of Drugs is preparing to give its recommendation to the Home Secretary soon that ecstasy be downgraded from A to B.

I'm never sure which is more arbitrary – the fashion for uppers or downers that changes wildly with each generation of drug-users, or the fashion in policy-making circles

By Andy Hayman

for downgrading one year and upgrading the next. We need to scrap the whole classification process – it is outdated, not understood by the public and utterly irrelevant to life on the streets.

I used to serve on the council in my capacity as the leading police officer on drugs policy. By the end

of my stint I felt that its detachment from grassroots reality had eroded its credibility. Its purpose seemed to be to generate endless rounds of meetings and glossy reports to send to ministers.

Up to 70 members – made up of representatives from all sorts of Government and voluntary bodies – attended the unwieldy full meetings, which were supported by a plethora of smaller working groups and subcommittees. I was always struck by how the experience of those living in the thick of the drugs problem got lost among the grey suits having highbrow technical and medical discussions. Although street-workers are represented, the actual men and women who work closely with dependent users do not attend.

The council would be horrified to learn that its recommendations on drugs classification are not taken seriously. But that is the case. The public either don't understand the process or are not interested in it. For the police, the advisory council is a sideshow; officers prefer to apply their professional discretion on whether to caution or arrest suspects.

Cannabis is so prevalent that how it is policed is dictated by manpower and resources – there is simply not enough time to push high numbers of offenders through the system

Put bluntly, how a drug is classified doesn't help police officers in their day-to-day duties. The first thought of an officer confronted by a user of an illegal drug is to weigh up whether the possession warrants anything more than a caution. To make an arrest and charge doesn't guarantee a prosecution so it may be simpler to deal with it on the street. That decision is made regardless of the classification of the drug involved.

For the courts, categorising a drug does help to provide a tariff for punishment. But even that idea has become dated as the Crown Prosecution Service now tends to apply its own prosecution guidelines. In practice, the classification of a drug does not significantly change how the courts or police deal with drug offenders.

This is well illustrated by the moves to reclassify cannabis and ecstasy. The upgrading of cannabis is presumably intended to trigger a

tougher enforcement policy towards its users and dealers.

Conversely, the downgrading of ecstasy sends a message to encourage a more relaxed approach. But past evidence suggests that life on the streets and in the courts will not change.

Cannabis is so prevalent that how it is policed is dictated by manpower and resources – there is simply not enough time for the police or the courts to push high numbers of offenders through the system. Regardless of the advisory council's rulings, the police and courts take a more lenient view towards users of cannabis because they deem it as less harmful than other drugs. I expect those same people will judge ecstasy to still be a dangerous drug. Reclassification will change nothing.

It is time to abandon any form of categorisation – regardless of their classifications, they are all illegal drugs and the powers of the police to deal with each type hardly differ. To varying degrees each category carries the power to arrest and search a suspect or premises. If the minor differences were ironed out and police were given the same powers to deal with all drug offences this would be a simple message to convey to the public.

Setting the tariffs for punishment is even simpler. The courts already apply

their own criteria for sentencing across a range of drug offences. Each case is considered on its own merits, aligning the crime with the punishment. If the courts required help in setting a tariff, a medical guide could be provided. This does not require the protracted and expensive classification process conducted by a large committee working at public expense.

After all, no equivalent body to the advisory council meets to provide technical advice to the courts for other types of criminal offending.

The classification of drugs matters only to the council and politicians – it is an irrelevance to the police and to other drug agencies. The decision by Jacqui Smith, the present Home Secretary, to reverse David Blunkett's downgrading of cannabis hints more of a political ping-pong match than anything more serious. More effort is directed towards debating how a drug should be classified than to trying to stem the misuse of drugs.

Rather than soldiering on trying to make a classification process that was designed in 1971 work in 2009, we should drop the pretence that classification matters.

Andy Hayman was Assistant Commissioner for Special Operations at Scotland Yard.

This article first appeared in the Times, *27 January 2009.*

© *Andy Hayman*

The big question

Is it time the world forgot about cannabis in its war against drugs?

Why are we asking this now?

Because yesterday a British think-tank published a report for next year's United Nations Strategic Drug Policy Review, suggesting that a decriminalised, regulated market in cannabis would cause less harm than the prohibition of the drug currently in force across most of the world.

What is the UN review?

It is an examination of progress made since the international community, at a special session of the UN General Assembly in New York in June 1998, agreed a ten-year programme of activity for the control of illegal drug use and markets – the 'war on drugs'. It is thought unlikely that enormous progress will be reported in 2009, as many drugs are purer, cheaper, and more widely available than ever before. Experts on drug policy are therefore looking again at the alternative to prohibition which is always in the background, but which no office-holding politician hoping for re-election appears able to contemplate – legalisation.

What exactly is the think-tank report?

It is the Global Cannabis Commission report, launched at a conference in the House of Lords yesterday and prepared for the Beckley Foundation, a charitable trust 'set up to promote the investigation of consciousness and its altered states from the perspectives of science, health, politics and history'. The report, put together by a specially-commissioned international group of academics and experts in drug policy analysis, attempts to put the issue of cannabis in a global perspective with a comprehensive view of the evidence, so that governments can move beyond what is termed 'the present stalemate in cannabis policy'.

Which stalemate is this?

Cannabis is used worldwide by 'a conservatively estimated 160m

By Michael McCarthy

people', according to the report, so it can hardly be said that prohibiting it is successful – and increasingly, nations cannot agree on the way forward. Some countries take a hard line – in the US, about three-quarters of a million citizens are arrested every year for cannabis possession – while other countries have considerably relaxed their penalties or their enforcement policies. (Until recently Britain could have been put into this category. Four years ago we downgraded dope from a class B to a class C drug – until in May, the Home Office, clearly at Gordon Brown's behest and in the face of official advice to the contrary, retightened the policy and made it class B once again, after fears in some quarters that stronger versions of the drug were leading to more harmful effects.) But internationally, cannabis is considered an outlawed substance, so changing the official regime is everywhere difficult.

Why does the report suggest cannabis should be legalised?

It argues that although cannabis can have a damaging effect on health and on mental health, it is actually far less damaging than alcohol and tobacco. 'Historically, there have only been two deaths worldwide attributed to cannabis, whereas alcohol and tobacco together are responsible for an estimated 150,000 deaths per annum in the UK alone,' the report alleges.

Much of the harm associated with cannabis use is 'the result of prohibition itself, particularly the social harms arising from arrest and imprisonment,' the report says, claiming that policies which control cannabis, whether draconian or liberal, appear to have little impact on the prevalence of consumption. It offers the alternative of a legal but properly regulated market.

'In an alternative system of regulated availability, market controls such as taxation, minimum age requirements, labelling and potency limits are available to minimise the harms associated with cannabis use,' it says, claiming that through a regulated market young people could be protected from the increasingly potent forms of the drug, such as skunk.

Wouldn't the legalisation of cannabis pave the way to the legalisation of all drugs?

It might well do, which is why, no matter what the relative harm of dope may be compared to cigarettes or whisky, a move to end prohibition would be stoutly resisted by opponents of liberalising the drug laws, and welcomed by those who would like to see liberalisation brought in. For it is the issue of prohibition itself, rather than the issue of cannabis, which is really at the heart of the argument. The drugs-liberalisation pressure group Transform yesterday welcomed the Global Cannabis Commission's call for legalisation, but said it would also welcome its now being applied to heroin and cocaine.

Much of the harm associated with cannabis use is 'the result of prohibition itself, particularly the social harms arising from arrest and imprisonment'

Why is prohibition at the heart of the argument?

Simple economics, say its opponents. It is simply a matter of supply and demand. If you squeeze the supply of a much-desired commodity – especially an addictive one – its price will rise sharply, and in an unregulated market, it can go sky-high. It then becomes too expensive for addicts to buy, and so they turn to crime or social deviancy on a large scale to feed their habits – burglary, shoplifting, prostitution. At the international scale, the profits are such that the trade is taken over by organised crime and whole countries are destabilised.

So just how big are the profits?

Transform's Danny Kushlick says: 'In the cocaine and heroin trade, the profit margin is anything between 2,000 and 3,000 per cent, which enables organised criminals to turn

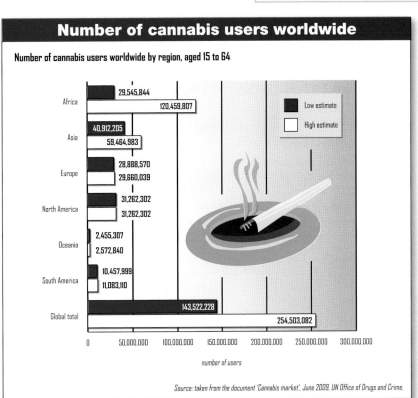

Number of cannabis users worldwide

Number of cannabis users worldwide by region, aged 15 to 64

Region	Low estimate	High estimate
Africa	29,545,844	120,459,807
Asia	40,912,205	59,464,983
Europe	28,888,570	29,660,039
North America	31,262,302	31,262,302
Oceania	2,455,307	2,572,840
South America	10,457,999	11,083,110
Global total	143,522,228	254,503,082

number of users

Source: taken from the document 'Cannabis market', June 2009. UN Office of Drugs and Crime.

what are effectively vegetables into commodities worth literally more than their weight in gold.' A large number of prominent and entirely respectable economists have bought this argument, and insist that drugs prohibition is entirely counter-productive, just as alcohol prohibition was in the US in the 1920s – until it was eventually repealed.

They range from Milton Friedman, the US guru of the free market, to Adair Turner, former director-general of the Confederation of British Industry, current chairman of the Government's Climate Change Committee and forthcoming chairman of the Financial Services Authority. A lot of senior scientists are also strongly in favour of drugs legalisation.

Wouldn't the legalisation of cannabis or indeed any drug just lead people down the path to addiction?

That is certainly the position of its opponents; it is more or less the position of the Government and of the Tory opposition. Economists might be in favour; politicians are very wary of legalising drugs. There seems to be no widespread popular call for it. Its proponents say that although more people might become drug users, the harm done would be far less than the

benefit gained by taking the world's Mafias and local criminals out of the equation.

So what are the chances that cannabis will cease to be internationally outlawed?

With the US running the show? Don't hold your breath.

Should cannabis be legalised on a world scale?

Yes...
⇨ It would immediately take the supply of the drug out of the hands of violent criminal syndicates.
⇨ Compared to alcohol and tobacco, which are freely available, cannabis is not very harmful anyway.
⇨ Any increased use of the drug would be greatly outweighed by the benefits gained.

No...
⇨ It would be a first step to more widespread, and potentially disastrous, liberalisation of other drugs.
⇨ It would lead to a great increase in use, which might put people on a 'slippery slope' to harder drugs.
⇨ Some forms of cannabis are very harmful and have been implicated as a cause of mental health problems.

First published 3 October 2008
© *The Independent*

⇨ Cannabis is the most widely used illegal drug in Britain. (page 1)

⇨ Cannabis is illegal; it's a class B drug. (page 1)

⇨ Drug driving is as illegal as drink driving. You could go to prison, get a heavy fine or be disqualified. (page 2)

⇨ The compound that gives cannabis its mind-altering properties is delta-9-tetrahydrocannabinol, known as THC. (page 3)

⇨ 20- to 24-year-olds are the age group most likely to have used cannabis in the past year. (page 4)

⇨ Approximately four per cent of the world's adults – some 162 million people – use cannabis at least once in the course of a year, making it the world's most widely-used illicit drug. (page 6)

⇨ Concern about the psychiatric effects of cannabis use outweighs concern for the drug's physical toxicity, and largely underpins its continuing illegality, including the recent UK decision to reclassify it. (page 7)

⇨ *Cannabis sativa* and *cannabis indica* are members of the nettle family that have grown wild throughout the world for centuries. Both plants have been used for a variety of purposes including hemp to make rope and textiles, as a medical herb and as the popular recreational drug. (page 9)

⇨ The amount of the main psycho-active ingredient, THC, that you get in herbal cannabis varies hugely, from as low as 1% up to 15%. The newer strains, including skunk, can have up to 20%. (page 11)

⇨ Research by North Staffordshire academics found there were no rises in cases of schizophrenia or psychoses diagnosed in the UK over nine years, during which the use of cannabis had grown substantially. (page 12)

⇨ Researchers at the Institute of Psychiatry at King's College London (KCL) have found that people who smoke skunk, the most potent form of cannabis available in the UK, are almost seven times more likely to develop psychotic illnesses than those who use traditional cannabis resin (hash) or grass. (page 13)

⇨ A new study published by University of Leicester researchers has found 'convincing evidence' that cannabis smoke damages DNA in ways that could potentially increase the risk of cancer development in humans. (page 14)

⇨ Cannabis was first made illegal in 1928. (page 15)

⇨ Cannabis has been used for centuries for medicinal purposes. It has even been claimed that Queen Victoria was prescribed the drug to relieve period pain. (page 16)

⇨ A recent Home Office study revealed that herbal cannabis accounted for 81% of all cannabis seized by the police on the street when giving a warning to users. Significantly, 97% of the herbal was sinsemilla or 'skunk'. Cannabis resin used to be much more popular (70% in 2002) than herbal cannabis. (page 17)

⇨ Cannabis first became popular in the West in the 1960s, when its use emerged as part of the general youth rebellion of that decade. (page 18)

⇨ Cannabis use has become a 'normal' part of young people's lives in many Western countries: up to 50% of people born after 1980 have at least tried it. (page 20)

⇨ Cannabis has changed dramatically since the 1970s. New methods of production such as hydroponic cultivation have increased the potency and the negative effects of tetrahydrocannabinol (THC), the most psychoactive of the chemical substances found in marijuana. (page 22)

⇨ Cannabis has been used for more than 4,000 years, including for medicinal purposes in Indian, Chinese and Middle-Eastern civilisations. In China, it has been used to treat such conditions as malaria, constipation and rheumatism. (page 25)

⇨ The British Lung Foundation estimates that smoking three to four joints a day causes the same level of damage as smoking 20 cigarettes a day. (page 28)

⇨ If the police think that you are dealing cannabis, they will arrest you. If you are convicted of supplying or intending to supply cannabis, you can be sentenced to a maximum of 14 years in prison and given an unlimited fine. If you sell cannabis near schools, you can get a stiffer prison sentence. (page 30)

⇨ Thousands of people would need to stop using cannabis in order to prevent a single case of schizophrenia, according to a new study from the University of Bristol. (page 31)

⇨ There is a substantial amount of anger over the Government's decision to reclassify cannabis, a politics. co.uk poll suggests. 13 per cent of respondents agreed with the decision, compared to 87 per cent who said they 'disagreed' or 'strongly disagreed'. (page 31)

⇨ The Government is currently spending £1.5 billion a year on its drugs policy. (page 35)

GLOSSARY

Cannabis

Cannabis is the most widely used illegal drug in Britain. Made from parts of the cannabis plant, it's a naturally occurring drug. It is a mild sedative (often causing a chilled-out feeling or actual sleepiness) and it's also a mild hallucinogen (meaning users may experience a state where they see objects and reality in a distorted way and may even hallucinate). The main active compound in cannabis is tetrahydrocannabinol (THC). Slang names include dope, ganja, grass, hash, marijuana, weed and pot.

Cannabis oil

This is made by separating the resin from the cannabis plant using various solvents. It is a sticky, dark honey-coloured oil.

Gateway theory

This refers to the idea that cannabis users are more likely to progress to harder drugs such as heroin. This theory is hotly debated: it is true that most people who use heroin have previously used cannabis, but only a small proportion of those who try cannabis then go on to use heroin.

Herbal cannabis (grass or weed)

This is made from the dried leaves and flowering parts of the female plant and looks like tightly packed dried herbs.

Medicinal cannabis

There is evidence that cannabis use alleviates the painful symptoms of some diseases, such as Multiple Sclerosis and Arthritis. This is a controversial subject, as many believe those with debilitating illness should not be prosecuted if they are using cannabis for pain relief. However, others say that the law must apply to everyone or its impact is weakened.

Mental health

There is some evidence that cannabis use can result in negative mental health outcomes. In the short term, it can cause paranoia, and for those with a pre-existing mental illness such as schizophrenia, it can contribute to a relapse. In addition, those with a family background of mental illness may be at increased risk of developing a psychotic illness through cannabis use.

The 'munchies'

A term sometimes used to describe the hunger pangs which are often experienced while using cannabis.

Reclassification

There are three categories of illegal substance, classes A, B and C, and drugs are classified according to how harmful they are known to be to users and society. Class A drugs are considered to be the most dangerous, and use or supply of these substances will incur a harsher criminal penalty. Class C drugs are the least harmful, but are nevertheless considered dangerous enough to be illegal. Cannabis was reclassified in 2004 from a class B to a class C drug. However, in 2008 it was again reclassified back to class B. On both occasions, reclassification has been hotly debated.

Resin (hash)

'Hash' is a blackish-brown lump made from the resin of the cannabis plant. In the past, this was the commonest form of cannabis in the UK, but this is no longer the case. Herbal cannabis (and especially powerful skunk strains) is now the most common form of cannabis used in the UK.

Sativex

A cannabis-based pain relief medicine administered as an oral spray. It is currently taken by around 1,200 people with MS in the UK.

Sinsemilla

A bud grown in the absence of male cannabis plants which has no seeds.

Skunk

This is a high-strength herbal cannabis. There is evidence that skunk has been increasing in THC content over the past three decades, resulting in stronger, more harmful cannabis. While previously resin was more common, skunk now dominates the UK cannabis market. Although the term 'skunk' was originally applied to specific strains of strong-smelling herbal cannabis, the term is now often applied to any type of very potent herbal cannabis.

THC

THC is an abbreviation of delta-9-tetrahydrocannabinol. This is the main psychoactive ingredient in cannabis and leads to the feeling of being 'stoned'. The higher the concentration of this chemical, the more potent the strain of cannabis. It is because of this ingredient that cannabis is one of the most easily detectable drugs when carrying out drugs tests, as THC can take weeks to clear from the body.

INDEX

Additional Resources

Other Issues titles

If you are interested in researching further some of the issues raised in *Cannabis Use*, you may like to read the following titles in the **Issues** series:

⇨ Vol. 187 *Health and the State* (ISBN 978 1 86168 528 5)

⇨ Vol. 176 *Health Issues for Young People* (ISBN 978 1 86168 500 1)

⇨ Vol. 163 *Drugs in the UK* (ISBN 978 1 86168 456 1)

⇨ Vol. 145 *Smoking Trends* (ISBN 978 1 86168 411 0)

⇨ Vol. 143 *Problem Drinking* (ISBN 978 1 86168 409 7)

⇨ Vol. 141 *Mental Health* (ISBN 978 1 86168 407 3)

⇨ Vol. 125 *Understanding Depression* (ISBN 978 1 86168 364 9)

⇨ Vol. 100 *Stress and Anxiety* (ISBN 978 1 86168 314 4)

For more information about these titles, visit our website at www.independence.co.uk/publicationslist

Useful organisations

You may find the websites of the following organisations useful for further research:

⇨ **Arthritis Research Campaign:** www.arc.org.uk

⇨ **Beckley Foundation:** www.beckleyfoundation.org

⇨ **Behind the Medical Headlines:** www.behindthemedicalheadlines.com

⇨ **Centre for Policy Studies:** www.cps.org.uk

⇨ **European Union:** http://europa.eu

⇨ **FRANK:** www.talktofrank.com

⇨ **Home Office Scientific Development Branch:** http://scienceandresearch.homeoffice.gov.uk

⇨ **Institute of Psychiatry, King's College London:** www.iop.kcl.ac.uk

⇨ **politics.co.uk:** www.politics.co.uk

⇨ **Royal College of Psychiatrists:** www.rcpsych.ac.uk

⇨ **TheSite:** www.thesite.org

⇨ **United Nations Office on Drugs and Crime:** www.unodc.org

⇨ **University of Leicester:** www.le.ac.uk

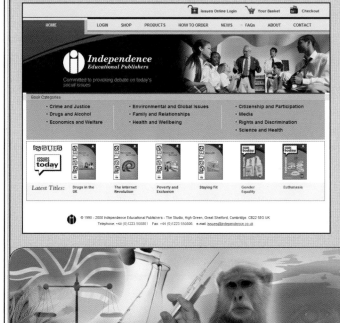

ACKNOWLEDGEMENTS

The publisher is grateful for permission to reproduce the following material.

While every care has been taken to trace and acknowledge copyright, the publisher tenders its apology for any accidental infringement or where copyright has proved untraceable. The publisher would be pleased to come to a suitable arrangement in any such case with the rightful owner.

Chapter One: The Effects of Cannabis

Cannabis, © Crown copyright is reproduced with the permission of Her Majesty's Stationery Office, *Cannabis controversy,* © Adfero, *Risks of cannabis use,* © United Nations Office on Drugs and Crime, *Impact of cannabis on bones 'changes with age',* © Arthritis Research Campaign, *Behind the medical headlines,* © RCPE and RCPSG 2009, *Cannabis and mental health,* © Royal College of Psychiatrists, *Schizophrenia link to cannabis denied,* © Staffordshire Sentinel News & Media Ltd, *Skunk 'poses greatest risk of psychosis',* © Institute of Psychiatry, King's College London, *'Cannabis alters DNA',* © University of Leicester, *Cannabis and your health,* © TheSite.org, *Medicinal use of cannabis,* © Adfero, *Marijuana use around the world,* © Beckley Foundation, *The world drugs problem, ten years on,* © European Union, *Home Office cannabis potency study 2008,* © Crown copyright is reproduced with the permission of Her Majesty's Stationery Office, *Why does cannabis potency matter?,* © United Nations Office on Drugs and Crime, *The families torn apart by teenage skunk epidemic,* © Guardian Newspapers Ltd 2009, *Helpline tells children 'pot safer than alcohol',* © Telegraph Group Ltd, London 2009, *Cannabis and the risks,* © Dr Mark Porter.

Chapter Two: Cannabis and the Law

Cannabis: the law has changed, © Crown copyright is reproduced with the permission of Her Majesty's Stationery Office, *Cannabis and psychosis,* © University of Bristol, *Poll reveals anger at cannabis law,* © Adfero, *David Nutt: my views on drugs classification,* © Guardian Newspapers Ltd 2009, *Politicians intoxicated by cowardice in drugs debate,* © Guardian Newspapers Limited 2009, *The phoney war on drugs – summary,* © Centre for Policy Studies, *The streets don't care what class drugs are,* © Andy Hayman, *The big question,* © The Independent.

Photographs

Stock Xchng: pages 2 (shin0); 16 (Gerhard Taatgen jr.); 17 (some.old. nobody); 19 (B S K); 21 (Tony Clough); 34 (ShivaHead); 35 (Vangelis Thomaidis).
Wikimedia Commons: pages 7 (Chmee2); 11 (Ryan Bushby); 30 (public domain); 34 (public domain).

Illustrations

Pages 1, 15, 26, 37: Don Hatcher; pages 5, 14, 25, 33: Simon Kneebone; pages 12, 18: Bev Aisbett; pages 13, 20, 29, 38: Angelo Madrid.

And with thanks to the team: Mary Chapman, Sandra Dennis, Claire Owen and Jan Sunderland.

Lisa Firth
Cambridge
January, 2010